CONTENTS

KU-054-959

AUTHOR'S NOTE

I hope that you enjoy this walk as much as I did both in the research and the preparation, as well as the walking of 1066 Harold's Way- three times!

In writing 1066 Harold's Way, I would like to thank my wife Stef for 'enjoying' every step of this walk during waking hours and the encouragement of our daughters Alex and Hannah and son in law Sean. To all the 1066 Walkers, Alex, Hannah, Sean, Fran, Gemma, Jim, Louise, Lynn, Mark, Mike, Sharon and the Northiam group who accompanied me during 2012 and walked some or all of the 100 miles from Westminster Abbey to Battle Abbey – they were all good days, even when it rained.

Thanks also to the many pubs and inns along the way that gave us a warm welcome and helped to toast 1066 Harold's Way - it will be good to return and visit you again.

I would also like to add my thanks to Rupert Matthews of Bretwalda Books and all the people and organisations who have given me their support, advice and encouragement, and to any that I have mistakenly omitted, for without them my dream of creating, writing and publishing 1066 Harold's Way would not have been fulfilled.

David Clarke
St Leonards-on-Sea, 2013

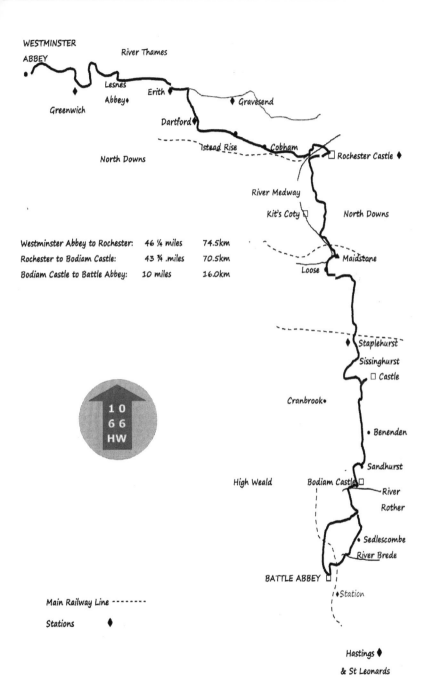

WESTMINSTER
ABBEY   River Thames

Greenwich   Lesnes
               Abbey◆   Erith◆   ◆ Gravesend

                    Dartford◆

North Downs   Istead Rise   ● Cobham
                                          ▢ Rochester Castle ◆

                         River Medway

                    Kit's Coty ▢   North Downs

Westminster Abbey to Rochester: 46 ¼ miles   74.5km
Rochester to Bodiam Castle: 43 ¾ miles   70.5km   Maidstone
Bodiam Castle to Battle Abbey: 10 miles   16.0km
                                          Loose

                                                    ◆ Staplehurst

                                                    Sissinghurst
                                                    ▢ Castle

                                          Cranbrook●

                                                    ● Benenden

                                                    Sandhurst
            1
            0   High Weald   Bodiam Castle▢
            6   ─River
            6
            HW   Rother

                                                    ● Sedlescombe
                                                    River Brede

                         BATTLE ABBEY ▢
                                        ◆ Station

Main Railway Line ---------

Stations   ◆
                                          Hastings ◆
                                          & St Leonards

INTRODUCTION

There were arrows everywhere. Long arrows, short arrows, broad and narrow arrows, even red and blue arrows.

I was in the bookshop at Battle Abbey and every map in every book that I looked at about the Battle of Hastings gave a different view of the route that Harold took from London.

There were arrows on a diagonal from London, aiming at Battle, four or five in a row as if a hail of arrows had been fired at William. There was a broad arrow creating a swathe across the south-east as the Saxon army passed over the land. Arrows approached Battle from all the points of the compass – except the south!

The artist in me liked the map that showed the more curved arrows from Westminster to Rochester and south towards Battle but this would have been a longer journey, over 90 miles rather than the 65 miles of the direct route and Harold was in a hurry. I read on before embarrassment set in and I bought the book.

The Weald was a forest in Saxon times and hacking a way through the trees and over the highest parts of the Downs and the Weald, through Tonbridge and Tunbridge Wells would have been a real struggle for the army. Even in the 18th century the Weald was declared 'roadless' and any journey took hours through the deepest clay imaginable (Cobbett). The Weald was not a traveller's paradise.

With the Roman roads still being used in Saxon times, there was a certain logic to the longer route – it followed the old Roman roads for much of the way and was a clear route through the forest. It is also legend that Harold's army camped overnight at Rochester on 11th October. 1066 Harold's Way would follow the old Roman roads through history.

I would be 60 the following year and the germ of an idea was planted, tended and encouraged by my wife until Harold rather took over for the summers of 2009, 2010 and 2011.

I began to research the possibility of a walk that followed Harold's route from London to Battle – the more I researched

The Battle site, looking down on the Normans, from the terrace at Battle Abbey

the more feasible it became – a pilgrimage to Harold, a challenge or just a good walk through history.

There was some poetic licence in first planning this walk. We can only presume as to the route that Harold took from London to meet his fate near Hastings. Apart from the major roads, that followed the lines of the old Roman roads, the rest were muddy tracks through the wide ranging forests of the Andreasweald. As a result, there is a belief that Harold used the Roman roads from London to Hastings.

1066 Harold's Way roughly follows the direction of the old Roman roads east out of London to Rochester and then tracks the Roman road south through Maidstone to Staplehurst and Bodiam, east of the present A229.

It is likely that Harold then approached Caldbec Hill from the north, along the line of the A2100, although there is the suggestion of an alternative via Sedlescombe. This route used the presumed Roman road from the iron quarries around Beaufort Park to the dock at Bodiam but it would suffer from delays in the crossing of the tidal estuary at Sedlescombe, now the River Brede.

1066 Harold's Way only deviates from this Roman route where necessary, to avoid the effects of the 'car', to follow a generally more scenic and historical route or to find a good pub. The modern Watling Street is just too dangerous for walkers!

1066 Harold's Way is certainly not meant to be historically accurate, there is much conjecture as to the actual march. However, it traces an important route through English history from the Stone Age to the present time.

If you look at a modern day road map it is fairly easy to follow the A2 to Rochester, south on the A229, through Maidstone which becomes the B2244 after Hawkhurst. A good driving route but not the one that we will follow!

Perhaps in Roman times, Watling Street would have proved as troublesome for traffic as the modern A2, heavy duty transport wagons that could only crawl at a snail's pace took up most of the road and were difficult to pass and chariots backed up as far as the eye could see. The air might have been a lot cleaner but the price of fuel would have still been a topic of conversation.

Sounds familiar – one solution, for the Romans, was to allow the wagons to only travel at night – that eased some of the congestion.

By 1000, if not before, London Bridge had been rebuilt and in 1066, Watling Street was still a major road but less well maintained then in Roman times - passable with care and certainly suitable for an army. Today, it is less of a joy to follow these old Roman roads through London.

1066 Harold's Way is 100 miles long (160km) and our journey will take 10 days rather than the 3 days of forced marching some 940 years ago.

In 1066, the Roman route totalled 68 miles (109km) - 33 miles (53km) to Rochester and 35 miles (56.5km) from Rochester to

Caldbec Hill. We know of one camp, at Rochester, on the night of 11th October and that the Army rendezvoused at the Hoar Apple Tree on 13th October. I imagine that they stopped again on route perhaps somewhere between Sissinghurst and Bodiam or at Bodiam itself as it would take time to cross this arm of the tidal Appledore estuary.

Daily mileage, for Harold's Way, is loosely based around 10 miles (16km) – about 4 hours of walking – but it is up to you to plan your daily dose in accordance with fitness, how you feel, transport links and whether there is a welcoming diversion on the path where you could spend a little time to reflect on 1066 Harold's Way.

Each Chapter is based around the excellent public transport links in South-East England. The walks are accessible for all those living in the South-East and London and were especially convenient for me living in St Leonards-on-Sea. Public transport also makes for an enjoyable walk, with time to explore and the odd pint at the end, without the difficulties faced with the need for two cars and parking.

For accommodation, I preferred to stay in historic Rochester for the first part of the walk. There is a main line rail link to London Bridge, a pleasant stroll to Westminster Abbey for the start and easy connections to both Greenwich, Lesnes Abbey and Dartford.

Greenhithe was just a couple of stations away and there are connections to Maidstone by bus and train taking us up to the start of Chapter Seven.

The next two walks, Chapters Eight and Nine are along the route of the Arriva No 5 Service, Maidstone to Sandhurst. In Chapter Nine, 1066 Harold's Way passes through Sandhurst, on route to Bodiam Castle, and you could decide to split this walk in two.

For the final base I would suggest either Hastings or St Leonards-on-Sea. Cross Country Service 349 from Hastings Station passes through Sedlescombe, Bodiam and Sandhurst and links with Arriva 5 at Hawkhurst. There are easy bus and

Cray Marshes wild and desolate

rail connections to and from Battle to allow you to celebrate the end of 1066 Harold's Way in style. *(See Appendix 4 for links to Accommodation and Appendix 1 for Travel Links)*

For each walk, I have identified the public transport links to take you to and from the start and finish points and places for food and refreshment. Such information would certainly have made Harold's journey a lot easier

These days Harold would have travelled from York by high speed train into King's Cross then the underground to Westminster. Perhaps it would be linked to a weekend Leisure Break, a trip to the theatre and a little light refreshment in a local hostelry. The horses would be replaced by mountain bikes. If Harold had to cope with The Elephant and Castle gyratory, the Old Kent Road, New Cross before even a sniff of countryside at Blackheath his Army would have been at a standstill before it even started and he would never had made his date with destiny and such a place in history.

For 1066 Harold's Way, our starting point will be Westminster Abbey, following the Embankment to cross the river at London Bridge and then continue on the Thames Path east towards Greenwich and the Thames Barrier.

I know that this is not rigidly adhering to Harold's route but it will be certainly a more enjoyable walk and there will still be plenty of 'history' to compensate for the lack of 'Harold'. Our link along the river is that Earl Godwin and Harold sailed up the Thames in 1052 to reclaim their place of power in the country and Harold's fleet returned to London in September 1066.

After Rochester we climb the chalk North Downs and here there once stretched the great British forest of Andreasweald *(Anderida-Roman)* covering most of central western Kent, central and north Sussex and south Surrey.

Our journey into history passes close to Iron Age Settlements, Stone Age relics at Kit's Coty and Roman villas such as that at Darenth. There are castles and cathedrals to see and key battle sites along the way that shaped the history of England.

In Kent and Sussex there are Roman roads and ancient pathways to walk, key ridgeway routes, tunnels through the trees and open land across the Weald. There is evidence of later sunken lanes, worn down by the heavy traffic of carts and wagons, washed away by the rain, 10' to 15' below the level of adjacent fields.

There is more than enough to stimulate the imagination.

1066 Harold's Way is a new walk not yet adopted as a long distance pathway and when walking the route, it was a joy to find well marked and well maintained paths with farmers providing clear routes across arable fields. It was not always the case. 1066 Harold's Way often follows little used older paths that are off the beaten track, revealing stiles and bridges in need of repair, paths overgrown or blocked with fallen trees, elusive or non-existent signage and arable fields with no clear route across. *(See Appendix 1 for links to report footpath problems)*

The more that the route is walked, and the problems reported, the greater the opportunity to improve and create a lasting memory to King Harold – one that I hope will continue to be walked until 2066 – now that is a challenge.

11th October 1066, Westminster Abbey

"Listen carefully. Cross London Bridge and turn left at Watling Street, it should be signposted Rochester, Canterbury and Dover. When you get to the big river and the old Roman bridge stop, the army will camp there the night. Tomorrow, turn right – south, along another Roman road to Maidstone and Bodiam. Wait for me there and we will cross the estuary together before meeting with the rest of our army at the Old Hoar Apple Tree, Caldbec Hill on the 13th.

Everybody knows where to meet and how to get there – good, off you go and be careful - we have a battle to fight. Don't get lost!"

The old Roman road to Caldbec Hill makes a lot of sense. There were few north-south routes through Kent and Sussex. The Romans had overcome the difficulties of the heavily forested Weald and built their road over the curving ridges, across the steep valleys and through the trees to connect their iron industry around Hastings with Watling Street.

It would make sense for these roads to be used throughout the Saxon period, and an easy route through the daunting Forest of Andreasweald.

Compare the 'good going' of the Roman roads to the alternative routes where a journey of six miles could take four hours along 'soft' roads through heavy clay - and that was in 1798. *(The Kent and East Sussex Weald, Peter Brandon)*

For the modern walker, the Andreasweald is not to be feared any more. We can look forward to the green lanes, cuttings, distinctive hollows and occasionally straight roads and imagine a time 1000 or even 2000 years ago.

It is not just the forest that has changed. The coastline was also very different in Roman and Saxon times.

The southern coastline around Rye and Winchelsea was dominated by the Appledore Estuary which stretched as far as

Bodiam and Sedlescombe. It was a key haven for ships on the South Coast with docks built along the navigable rivers Rother and Brede and ship building at Smallhythe and Appledore.

The Romans had created 'ports' where Bodiam and Sedlescombe are now. They built a causeway at Bodiam to make the crossing of the tidal River Rother easier but at Sedlescombe, the River Brede was too wide for a bridge or causeway and the only way to cross was by ferry. Harold would need to use both crossings if he were to arrive at Caldbec Hill on time.

This vast expanse of water created a natural hazard for both Harold and William. Harold had to find a way across for his army and for William, it proved a barrier to his desire to move on London. To break out of his beachhead at Hastings he needed to secure the key cross roads at Senlac Hill.

I do hope that you enjoy walking Harold's Way - I did.

Roman Roads in the South-East
There is a full description of the Roman Watling Street and the Roman Road Route 13, Rochester to Maidstone and Hastings in 'Roman Roads in Britain' by Ivan D Margary.

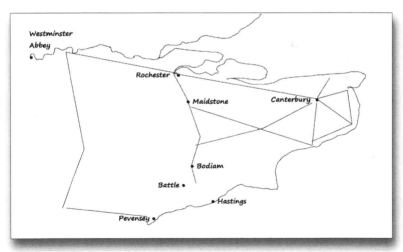

Harold's likely route

Watling Street from London to Rochester and Margary's Roman Route 13 south from Rochester, Maidstone, Staplehurst to the Appledore Estuary and what is now Bodiam.

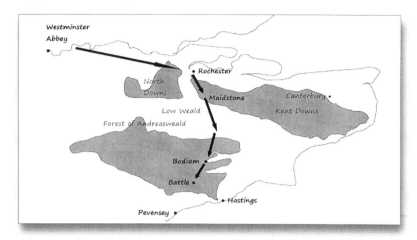

Coastline at the time of Harold

Harold would need to cross the River Rother at Bodiam and either march to Battle by Sedlescombe or the 'dry route' through Cripps Corner.

The coastline began to change after the great storms of the 14th century. Today's coastline is shown as ——

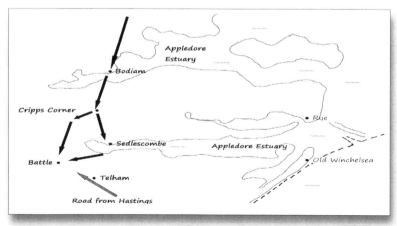

ENGLAND IN 1066

Edward the Confessor (King of England 1042 - 1065) dreamed of building a great monastery and abbey on an island in the Thames, up river and to the west of the City of London. The result was Westminster Abbey. A royal palace was built close to the Abbey the remains of which lie underneath the Houses of Parliament. Edward died almost as the Abbey was consecrated and it was his death and his succession, disputed between three rivals, that began the tumultuous history of 1066.

Harold, Earl of Wessex and probably the most powerful man in the country took the initiative and was crowned King of England in the new abbey on January 6th 1066. He set in motion a chain of events that led to the Battle of Stamford Bridge and

Westminster Abbey and the start of 1066 Harold's Way

ended with defeat at Hastings. William, Duke of Normandy, would be crowned King in the same Abbey on December 25, 1066.

The right of succession was complicated to say the least as King Edward died childless with no clear heir to the throne. However, Edward had married Harold's sister, Edith, so there was a family link for Harold to exploit but no bloodline. Harold, being on the spot, seized the opportunity to be crowned King. In opposition were Danes and Normans who both claimed and coveted the title of King of England and all that this green land possessed.

To understand the situation a little more, we now need to go back to the turn of the century, to a time when England was split between the Danish north and the Saxon south. Two kings, two capitals, two administrations and both Danes and Saxons claimed sovereignty over the country.

The Saxon King Ethelred's marriage to Emma of Normandy created an important alliance against the Danes. Battles and skirmishes continued up to Ethelred's death in April 1016, when Edmund Ironside, Ethelred's son by his first marriage, managed to create a temporary stalemate. It would not last long. Edmund was murdered in November the same year and in the void that followed, Danish Kings sat on the throne of England first Cnut (Canute) and then his sons Harold Harefoot (d. 1040) and Harthacnut (d. 1042). The dynasty that now ruled England would set down a bloodline for future claims to the throne. Believing himself to be Cnut's heir, it would be Harold Hardrada, the King of Norway, who would feature in the events of 1066.

Emma, Ethelred's widow, humiliatingly returned to Normandy with her sons, Alfred and Edward, carrying her disappointment, grievances and loss of status with her.

More intrigue and more political manoeuvrings followed. Cnut, now King of England, created an alliance with Normandy by marrying Emma fulfilling her ambition to once again be married to a King.

Whilst living in Normandy, Edward who would later assume the English throne in 1042 treated William as his heir and William expected to be named King of England in succession to Edward, conveniently ignoring any Danish claim to the throne.

Harold Godwinson, Earl of Wessex, had previously agreed to support William as King but reneged on this promise, claiming duress, and in 1065 sought to strengthen his own position with the failing King, Edward the Confessor.

In January 1066, all these promises and covenants were broken on the death of King Edward when Harold took the throne and violent confrontation became the order of the day as England prepared for war.

The Dane, Harald Hardrada and his army, in alliance with Harold's estranged brother Tostig, would attack through the North of England. Duke William prepared a fleet and an army to attack through the south. King Harold prepared for them both.

Early autumn saw the defeat and the loss of the Northern Army at the Battle of Fulford on 20th September 1066, a loss that would have a profound effect on the Battle of Hastings three weeks later. Harold had to move his army quickly to York to meet this northern threat and on 25th September 1066, King Hardrada and Tostig were defeated and killed at the Battle of Stamford Bridge and the north was secure again.

Then, word came that William and his army had landed at Pevensey on 28th September. Harold's march south to London from York became the stuff of legends and it was the second leg, from London to the south coast that forms the basis of 1066 Harold's Way. You could not write a better story.

When Harold arrived back from Stamford Bridge, London was the most prosperous and largest city in Britain, the capital and the official seat of Government. In 1066, the countryside and high moorlands were scarcely populated. Large areas were given over to forests, woodland, un-drained marsh or fen and the population concentrated in East Anglia and the eastern Midlands with the exception of London. Towns were small and often merged with the surrounding countryside and nearly all served only their limited regional area.

In the South-East, the Weald and the Forest of Andreasweald created a very difficult terrain in which to travel. Most of the ancient British trackways followed the high ridges of the Weald, east to west, with very few roads north to south – the direction in which Harold needed to travel to do battle with William. Roman roads in Britain had been so well built that even in 1066 they continued to be used. They were still seen as important communication links in Saxon England.

In 1066, the southern coastline was very different to what it is today. Tidal rivers filled the valleys that had to be crossed by Harold's large army. The route needed to be planned with care. The autumn nights were drawing in and the army needed to arrive at Caldbec Hill fresh enough to defeat the Norman army and drive them back into the sea. As for Harold's Army, we can imagine Saxon soldiers marching on wild and windswept ridges and dark and deserted green lanes dominated by great forests. On the 13th October 1066, after three days marching, Harold and his army met, as agreed, at the 'Old Hoar Apple Tree' on Caldbec Hill.

We will walk on these same ridges and along the same green lanes. We will walk over the North Downs, the High Weald and across the Wealden valley. We will cross the Medway and what is left of the Appledore Estuary, at Bodiam and Sedlescombe, and make the final climb up the hill to Caldbec and Senlac. We will share the history of 1066.

Harold's Timeline: Westminster Abbey to the Battle of Senlac Hill.

3 October: Harold and 1,000-1,500 troops return south from the battlefields of Stamford Bridge but without his allies, the defeated and destroyed Northern Army. It was yet another forced march for his army.

6 October: While his men continue on to London, Harold stops at Waltham Abbey to pray for victory. There have been attempts to resolve the situation diplomatically with messengers travelling between Harold and William but these negotiations fail.

11 October: Harold reaches London. He is impatient and gathers together as many troops as he can and sets out for the south coast to meet William. That night his army makes camp at Rochester.

13 October: Harold's army reaches Caldbec Hill, the rallying point, 7 miles from Hastings. By mid-afternoon William's scouts have spotted them.

14 October: Harold is defeated and killed by William on Senlac Hill now known as the Battle of Hastings. His body is so mutilated that he can only be identified by Edith Swan-Neck, his Danish-law wife, from markings on his chest known only by her!

Later: Saxon reinforcements arrive as the Battle of Hastings reaches its conclusion. They form a line of defence at 'The Malfosse', a deep and hidden ditch, and in this final skirmish inflict heavy losses on the rampaging Norman cavalry but it is too little, too late.

Battle of Hastings Re-enactment:

An annual re-enactment of the Battle of Hastings is held at Battle Abbey on the weekend closest to 14th October. Visit the English Heritage website for details: http://www.english-heritage.org.uk

1066 HAROLD'S WAY WALK 1:
WESTMINSTER TO GREENWICH ⟨🚶 Public Footpath⟩

Distance: 9 miles
Time: 3 hours
but allow up to 5 hours
Maps: OS Explorer 162
London A-Z
www.streetmap.co.uk

Travel: www.travelinesoutheast.org.uk
www.nationalrail.co.uk
Rail:
London Charing Cross, London Bridge,
Greenwich
www.southeasternrailway.co.uk
London Underground:
London Underground to Westminster
Transport for London
www.tfl.gov.uk
Water Bus
Thames Clipper
www.thamesclippers.com
Parking: Best to use public transport
London: Difficult and expensive
Greenwich: Pay and Display

Connecting Long Distance Paths:
The Thames Path National Trail
www.thames-path.org.uk
www.walklondon.org.uk/walk_finder.asp

Accommodation:
London, Greenwich, Rochester
Use any as a base and connect by train.
There is accommodation to suit every pocket.
Appendix 4: Tourist Information links

Refreshments: Pubs
The Angel
The Mayflower
Old Salt Quay
Blacksmiths Arms
Dog and Bell
Spanish Galleon Shepherd Neame
Old Brewery / Meantime Brewery
The Trafalgar

Surrey Docks Farm: café (Wed – Sun)
Island Gardens Café: opp. Greenwich
Various shops and pubs along the way and a
few personal suggestions in Appendix 3

Other Walks:
Maritime Rotherhithe History Walk
Jubilee Greenway

Geography
A Thames River walk.
Occasional detours through backstreets,
between old warehouses and riverside flats.

Path Profile & Difficulty
Flat, occasional steps.
Although an easy walking section on
pathways and roads, it is hard on the feet and
legs. Hard boots may not be the best option
and there is a need to ensure good hydration
and maintain the usual timed rest stops rather
than after specific miles - you could be on
your feet for five to six hours all told.

Reflections

I love the smell of London and the sights and sounds of a fresh new morning, the luxury of a coffee and a Danish at a pavement cafe and whilst others rush, I can think about the miles to walk to Greenwich and on to Battle. These days, the armies preparing for battle are tourists and their guides are their commanders with umbrellas for flags - a rallying point - trying to stem the tide of London preparing for work.

Below Tower Bridge there are the remnants of the once great London Docks that stretched for miles along both sides of the river, St Katherine's Dock, Limehouse Basin, Russia Dock, Greenland Dock and dominating the skyline - Canary Wharf. Now there are flats, development and re-development.

There are famous pubs to while away the hours and wharves that launched the ships of Captain Cook, the Pilgrim Fathers, Nelson and Drake. Recreate the scenes painted by Turner and Canaletto and take time to stand and stare at a London of a different age -imagine the noise, the smells, the people and the army. Was it wet or was it dry, sunny or cloudy or was an autumnal chill rising from the nearby river?

The Walk

Start at the West Entrance to Westminster Abbey, the door furthest away from the Houses of Parliament, where there is

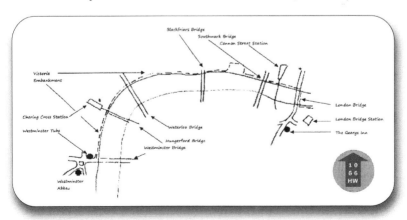

space away from the crowds at the North Door entrance. Walk towards the North Door and Parliament Square with the Houses of Parliament in front and head for the Tower of Big Ben. At the foot of Big Ben is a subway that will take you to Victoria Embankment for the start of the walk to London Bridge, east along the Thames and the Thames Path. In 1066, the road would have been slightly to the north to link up with the higher ground where the Strand is now.

The Thames has been revitalised since Harold's time and there will be no need to take the high ground.

Away from the crowds around Parliament Square and those on the South side around the London Eye, 1066 Harold's Way follows the north bank of the river. First, there are boats sailing to Greenwich from Westminster Pier but that would be too easy. A few more steps to reach the Battle of Britain memorial, not our battle but just as significant, fought out over south-east England.

There is so much to see at the start of 1066 Harold's Way and so much history along the Thames that you can easily be distracted from the task ahead. It is subjective but I found certain elements fascinating and worth a stop along the walk and for others, I will return to at a later date. We have nine miles to walk and cannot fit everything in.

The Victoria Embankment dates from 1870 and covered the new sewer for a healthier London, a cleaner Thames and the new District Line Underground. Gardens and walkways were created and the new road relieved the notorious congestion on The Strand and Fleet Street.

On the approach to Charing Cross Station, it is worth taking the time to cross the road and walk part way over the Hungerford footbridge. There is a wonderful view along to Westminster from here and little has changed since Monet painted his View of Westminster in 1871– good for a photograph.

Walk back down the steps of Hungerford Bridge and to the right is a tunnel, underneath the railway lines. It leads to the

Inspiration for Monet's Westminster

Embankment Gardens where we take a short detour left, up Villiers Street, towards The Strand and by Gordon's Wine Bar, is The Watergate on the right.

Gordon's Wine Bar, presumed to be the oldest wine bar in London, is well worth a visit and a delight to sit outside if the weather is good and you can find a table. Through the iron gate and down the steps into what was once a wharf on the north bank of the river. Into the park by the first gate and look back at the Watergate's lost magnificence, marooned in the Embankment Gardens, a large and now useless memorial to the Dukes of Buckingham. Before the Embankment was built, the river was much wider and The Watergate was once the private wharf for York House standing proud on the north bank of the Thames.

In 1747, close to here, Canaletto painted his view of the river with St Pauls in the background. With all the trees in the Embankment Gardens we will have to wait until Waterloo Bridge for a similar view to Canaletto.

Through the gardens and Canary Wharf comes into view, it will serve as a marker for the first part of this walk.

Back to the river and on to Waterloo Bridge. If you want to compare the 1747 view of the river with that of today climb the steps onto the Bridge and look towards St Pauls. Then the river flowed more to the north and was much wider with little building on the south side. Most likely the river ran a similar course in Harold's time.

Return to Victoria Embankment and continue east. The Shard on the South Bank, 1016ft high, arrows into the sky and transforms the South Bank. Underneath Blackfriars Bridge where every alley way still ends at the river and in the late 19th century boats and ships would have lined the Thames. Along St Pauls Walk and under the Millennium Bridge, with its glimpse of St Pauls up the steps to the left, to follow the Thames Path (Riverside Path East), away from the river. On the south side, there is a re-creation of Shakespeare's Globe Theatre.

Turn right and just round the corner is Stew Lane and the Samuel Pepys gastro-pub with its views over the river. Past Queen's Quay into Queenhithe and back to the river by the side of London's former dock, first mentioned in 899 and certainly

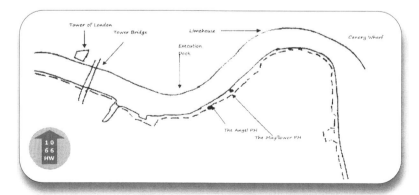

here in Harold's time. There are storyboards to relate the history of the area.

Continue along Three Barrels Walk into an area that formed the basis of Roman London, surrounded by walls, and re-occupied by the Saxons in the 9th century as a defence against Viking raids up the Thames.

Into Fruiterer's Passage and the subway under Southwark Bridge where there are tiled pictures showing some of the history of this bit of London – much later than Harold but of interest all the same.

Back onto Three Cranes Walk and past the site of the Three Cranes Stairs, one of a number of public stairs on the Thames at the beginning of the 18th century. They were once used by the watermen, barges, wherries and ferries but many of the stairs later disappeared as services declined as a result of competition from cabs, new bridges and steamboats as London developed in the 19th and 20th centuries.

In place of the watermen, we now have the fast Thames Clipper catamarans providing regular commuter and tourist transport along the river. Maybe they will ease our journey back from Greenwich to the Embankment and provide us with a different view of 1066 Harold's Way.

Left and then right, underneath Cannon Street Railway Bridge, into Hanseatic Walk to continue under London Bridge and then immediately turn left, up the steps to cross the River and join the Thames Path on the south side.

We are assuming that Harold crossed the Thames at London Bridge as we do. There has been a London Bridge on this site since Roman times and it was the only Bridge for centuries. Harold would have crossed here to the south side to connect with the route of the old Roman road, Great Dover Street and the beginning of Watling Street (the modern A2/M2).

Into Southwark, long the place to start or end a journey, a place for pilgrims, traders and travellers and the writers, Chaucer and Dickens. The George Inn is now Southwark's only surviving coaching inn rebuilt in 1676 and worth a visit, either now or later. It is just a short walk down Borough High Street, past Southwark Cathedral and Borough Market (open Thursday to Saturday, a delight for 'foodies' and with a couple of good pubs itself) – so much to keep you from 1066 Harold's Way. Have we time for visit? 6½ miles to Greenwich - perhaps another day.

Across the river is the Old Custom House, the Gherkin, St Pauls and a poetic view of the City skyline behind. This is Queens Walk with HMS Belfast moored by its side and framed by Tower Bridge. Over the river is The Tower of London and the White Tower built by William in 1078 - perhaps not something for us or Harold to dwell on now at the start of 1066 Harold's Way.

We are leaving the old Roman Road for the moment and using the Thames Path to Greenwich, historically incorrect but an altogether more peaceful route.

Walk under Tower Bridge and into Shad Thames. After around 50 metres, turn left into Butler's Wharf to reach the river again. The old warehouses, have been revitalised into London Living but the names are remembered in Shad, Butlers Wharf and others. Follow the Thames Path signs through Bermondsey and Rotherhithe.

Access to the river has always been difficult here with warehouses, docks and quays lining the river bank. A hundred and fifty years ago, there would have been the noise of ships being unloaded and wagons drawn, full of the cries of workmen and machinery but for us, it is quiet and peaceful now that we have left the crowds of the Embankment behind us.

The lanes are narrow and dwarfed by high walls, there is a darkness even during the day and when the tide is out and the mud revealed, in the side docks and creeks, there is a feeling of Dickens London about the place, maybe at the end of Oliver Twist - or is it just my imagination.

Into Rotherhithe and old docks converted for modern London. Continue into Bermondsey Wall West round into Chambers Street, turn left into Loftie Street to meet the river

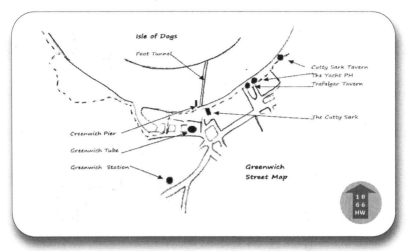

again and on to pass the Old Justice Inn with it's plaque to Sir Paul McCartney (an A-Z can be handy here). Walk along Bermondsey Wall East, past the site of Edward III's manor house to Cherry Garden Pier and The Angel PH.

It is said that the view from The Angel inspired Turner to paint the Fighting Temeraire as he watched the warship pass by on its final journey to the breaker's yard – no doubt it was from the inside of the pub rather than the outside with a quart of ale to help the imagination.

Wapping is on the opposite bank and Wapping New Stairs, with the water swirling around the beach, is the most likely site of Execution Dock. Pirates, thieves and mutineers were hanged and left for three tides to wash over them. You could drink and watch the hanging of the notorious pirate Captain Kidd on May 23rd 1701, safe across the river. Such events were seen as public holidays but the fun ended with the last hanging in 1830. Look out for a warehouse with the letter E on one wall, it stands on the site of Execution Dock. It is ironic that the very first River Police Station for the Marine Police was built close to Wapping New Stairs, in 1798.

After The Angel continue by the river until the path turns away into Rotherhithe Street and on the right is the Church of

27

St Mary the Virgin, built in 1715, to replace an earlier 12th century medieval church. There is a great deal of history about this church with connections to the Mayflower and the Pilgrim Fathers plus it has an excellent website.

Here, by the river in Rotherhithe, there is a sense of times past – there have been people living and working at the dock since Saxon times and I do feel that I am walking through history.

Next is the Mayflower PH, formerly 'The Shippe' of the 1600's, rebuilt in the 18th century and renamed as the 'Spread Eagle and Crown' until in 1957, it was finally restored and named The Mayflower. It was in 1620 that the Mayflower first set sail for America from a quay close to this spot.

It is 4½ miles from Westminster and halfway, perhaps it is time for a little 'rest' after all it does look a cosy pub ………. go on then, no will power – you will not be disappointed.

After the Mayflower is the Brunel Museum with its displays of the historic Thames Tunnel. Cumberland Wharf (with its sculpture 'Sunbeam Weekly and the Pilgrim's Pocket') leads to the entrance to Surrey Water and it's red rolling lift bridge installed in the 1950s. Follow the Thames Path signs past the Old Salt Quay PH, with just under 4 miles to go. Detour away from the river into Rotherhithe Street and back, opposite the Compass Alehouse.

On from Wapping and as you walk round the bend look across the river to Limehouse, a dock since medieval times and in the 19th and early 20th centuries it was a dangerous place to be. It was London's first and original China Town and the opium and gambling dens soon attracted more than just Chinese sailors. Dickens, Conan Doyle and Oscar Wilde all visited Limehouse and they secured its seedy and lurid history in popular imagination. It reputedly became the place for high adventure, fuelled by stories of the fictional Fu Manchu and Sherlock Holmes and all the 'dross' of the world.

We have the width of the river to protect us from our imagination. You can stand and stare across the river with

View of the Thames towards the City of London

'Limehouse Blues' playing in your ear and imagine the 1920's – there is a clip on You Tube http://www.youtube.com/watch?v=En7EGSxUbTM.

Then, Canary Wharf comes into view with the towers of its merchants and the wealthy striving to be ever higher in the sky, a modern San Gimignano.

For the first time, there is an openness about 1066 Harold's Way with a wide views over the Thames and I realise that I am looking forward to walking over the Weald and Downs of Kent and Sussex but there is a way to go first before I can leave London behind.

Leave the river, past the Blacksmith's Arms, (Fullers/Thai Food) and left through a gate to follow signs for the Thames Path that appear to take you to the Hilton Hotel reception. Further waymarks lead you through the car parks to rejoin the Thames. *Alternatively, walk past the enormous Hilton Hotel (built on the site of Nelson's dry dock) and then bear left back to the river to continue along the signposted Thames Path.*

Leave the river again by Surrey Docks Farm. If the farm is open you can continue the Thames Path through the farm, if not, follow Rotherhithe Street round to rejoin the river again along Vaughan Street.

This is the pattern of this walk as the riverside is blocked with yards and warehouses. At the vast expanse of Greenland Dock, there are barges moored here as house boats and later, at Allington Lock on the River Medway (Walk 6), we can see similar barges moored as a reminder of their Thames trading days.

A signpost shows 2¼ miles to go to Greenwich. Past the Dog and Duck Stairs and Greenland Pier, a stop for the Thames Clipper, and continue along Deptford Strand and the Thames Path. In front are the trees of Greenwich Park with the Observatory on the horizon. Here also, is the site of the Tudor dockyard, Drakes Steps and the Royal Victoria Victualling Yard.

The waterfront prevents continued access to the river and this final 1¼ miles is mostly through the former Victorian back streets of Deptford.

At the end of the buildings, turn right through the wonderful new playground and follow the winding path away from the river, through Pepys Park to Grove Street and turn left. Thames Path signage is a little sparse here and an A-Z can be useful – if in doubt, follow the signs for the National Cycle Route 4.

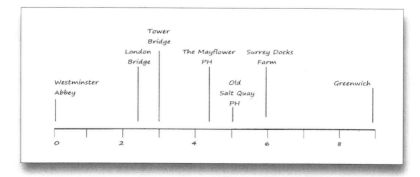

Follow the signs into Sayes Court Park, Sayes Court Street, left into Prince Street and at 'The Dog and Bell' (beer paradise), turn left and along Watergate Street for a final view of the river with its statuary of Tsar Peter the Great before following the path to cross Deptford Creek.

After the bridge, turn left into Norway Street and right at the bottom and suddenly, without fanfare, you are in Greenwich, in the square dominated by the Cutty Sark, with views over the Thames and the end of this section.

I left Westminster at lunchtime and, with all the sightseeing, it has taken most of the afternoon to walk here. Speed was not an issue, I did not have to meet the challenge of William. This will always be a slow section and for a relaxed walk, take the day, do not push on too hard and find the time to enjoy the finish – Greenwich is worth it.

They say that the best view of Greenwich is from across the Thames. The Greenwich Foot Tunnel will take you to Island Gardens for a cup of tea and West Indian food, at the Island Gardens café, a DLR station and most of all for a memorable photograph standing where Canaletto painted his 'View of Greenwich'.

Although the Thames Path was not on his 1066 route, the river still has such strong connections with Harold and the enormous history of the Thames goes a long way to make this section special. There are so many places to stop for refreshments and savour 1066 Harold's Way that you could indulge yourself with the comfort of public transport to take you back to London or on to Rochester.

I have listed a few favourites in Appendix 3 but please check opening hours to avoid disappointment. A London A-Z can be handy to save you getting lost. Later in Harold's Way, pubs can be a long way apart – savour them whilst you can.

The Thames Clipper at Greenwich Pier takes you back to London, the DLR is close or for a main line rail connection, allow at least 15 minutes to walk to the station on Greenwich High Road.

Information: for Weblinks, see Appendix 4 and www.1066haroldsway.co.uk
Westminster Abbey
Significant in the story of Harold and the events that led up to his coronation in
January 1066. For a more complete history, use the following link:
www.westminster-abbey.org/our-history
Houses of Parliament and Big Ben
This site was part of the Royal Palace established by Edward the Confessor and
subsequently enlarged by the Normans. It became increasingly used for government
from the 13thcentury. Today's Parliament buildings and Big Ben were built following
the great fire of 1834. www.parliament.uk/about/living-heritage/
Monet
'The Thames below Westminster' about 1871 (National Gallery)
Charing Cross Station
Built on the site of the old Hungerford Market and a 'blacking' factory where a 12
year old Dickens was sent to work.
Canaletto
Painted views of London many of which feature the Thames before the construction of
the Embankment – can be viewed from the internet:
- The Thames and City of London from Richmond House
- The Thames from the Terrace of Somerset House
- A View of Greenwich from the River
London Bridge.
Since the first Roman bridge, there have been many 'new' London Bridges with the
latest opened in 1973. It is feasible that Harold crossed here in 1066.
Southwark
South of London Bridge and formerly at the junction of the Roman Stane Street and
Watling Street, Southwark was linked to Roman roads throughout the South-East (see
'Roman Roads in Britain', Margary). It was been renowned for its inns; The Tabard
with Chaucer, The White Hart with Dickens (where he first introduces Sam Weller),
The Catherine Wheel and the George, all well known spacious 'hostelries' with
galleried courtyards to serve travellers and their horses. The George is the only
surviving inn and is well worth a visit, situated just a ¼ mile south from London
Bridge.
Tower of London
Built by Normans at the instigation of William so it was not here in 1066 as Harold
passed and outside this story. Wait for 1066 William's Way.
Tower Bridge
This iconic and symbolic bridge was completed in 1894 and outside our time frame.
However, there is no reason why you should not cross here if you wish
J. M. W. Turner (c.1775–1851).
The Fighting Temeraire,1839 (National Gallery) depicts the 98-gun HMS Temeraire
being towed towards its final berth in Rotherhithe to be broken up for scrap in 1838.
Church of St Mary the Virgin, Rotherhithe (www.stmaryrotherhithe.org/index.php)

The Angel PH, Rotherhithe Street

There has been a pub on this site since the 15thcentury when it was established by the monks of Bermondsey Priory. The oldest part overlooks the Thames and Execution Dock. Judge Jeffries watched the condemned hang across the River and it is believed that Turner gained the inspiration for the 'Fighting Temeraire' from the balcony.

Mayflower PH, Rotherhithe Street

In 1620, The Mayflower set sail for America, from a quay close to an inn called The Shippe. The story of the Pilgrim Fathers had begun. The Mayflower and its crew returned to Rotherhithe in 1621 and the Captain, Christopher Jones, died in 1622 and is buried in St. Mary's Churchyard, a plaque records his journey. Later, The Shippe was rebuilt, renamed The Spread Eagle and Crown and in 1957, restored and, in recognition of its historic connection with America, renamed The Mayflower. The pub was the post office for the river and is licensed to sell both US and British postage stamps with its pints. The custom may be re-instated in the future.

The Thames Tunnel

Designed by Marc Brunel, the Thames Tunnel was one of the greatest engineering feats of the 19th century. Running between Rotherhithe and Wapping it was the world's first tunnel under a navigable river.
http://news.bbc.co.uk/local/london/hi/people_and_places/history/newsid_8564000/8564653.stm

Maritime Rotherhithe History Walk: Granaries, Shipyards and Wharves.
I found this walk fascinating, described in great detail and with much historical content on the Southwark Borough website. Well worth the read even if you do not do the walk:
http://www.southwark.gov.uk/site/scripts/google_results.php?q=maritime+rotherhithe+history+walk

The Thames Path National Trail

The 'Walk London' site gives a comprehensive guide and added historical and geographical detail about this section of the Thames Path, from Westminster to Greenwich, and partly for Walks 2 and 3, continuing towards the Thames Barrier, Erith and the River Darent. The maps can be printed or downloaded and are excellent. These sections can be hard to follow as signage is not always obvious and there are occasions when we need to detour away from the river into the backstreets.
www.thames-path.org.uk   and   www.walklondon.org.uk/walk_finder.asp

Deptford

The name is taken from the OE for the deep ford that crossed the Ravensbourne but the Romans established their docks at Greenwich and rather by-passed Deptford.

Greenwich

The name derives from both the Roman and Saxon names for Greenwich, Grenovicum and Grenawic which mean green hamlet. The town has had a long and royal history for over 1000 years with links to Drake, Nelson, the Royal Naval College, the Cutty Sark and the Thames interwoven into its history. The river supplied the whitebait for the famous whitebait suppers that drew many political and literary figures to its dining

rooms in the 18th and 19th centuries and 'The Trafalgar' was a favourite haunt of Dickens. The Observatory is on the hill, there is a covered market and much to see and do to keep you occupied at the end of the first section of 1066 Harold's Way.
www.greenwich.gov.uk/Greenwich/LeisureCulture/Tourism/

Footnote: Approaching Bermondsey, I saw a young woman in jeans and with a daypack, following a similar route. I stopped for photographs and to enjoy the history and she moved in front and as she checked her map I passed her. Opposite Limehouse we stopped together. She was from Chicago, having an away day without the safety of the rest of her group and said "There is nothing much to see here – it's a bit boring, I expected more".

"There is all this history" I said enthusiastically. "Opposite is Limehouse, the China Town of old, the dross of the world docked here, opium dens, Sherlock Holmes and Doctor Fu-Manchu. You've passed Execution Dock where pirates were hanged, references to the Mayflower and the Pilgrim Fathers, the pub where Paul McCartney recorded music, the Kings Steps and Brunel and the last voyage of the Fighting Temeraire. The Saxon fleet sailed by here in 1066 before the Battle of Hastings. And when you get to Greenwich…"
She produced one of those little fold out maps of London.
"Oh, I expected all those Bridges, the Wheel and Big Ben, where am I?"
She turned and started the long hot walk back into tourism. I hope that she told the rest of her party of her journey into the unknown.

The Royal Naval College at Greenwich began life in 1694, underwent conversions in 1873 and left naval use in 1998. The magnificent buildings are now used for a variety of purposes.

34

1066 HAROLD'S WAY WALK 2:
GREENWICH TO LESNES ABBEY

Public Footpath

Distance: 9.75 miles
Time: 3½ hours
Maps: OS Explorer 162
London A-Z
www.streetmap.co.uk

Travel:
www.travelinesoutheast.org.uk
www.nationalrail.co.uk
www.tfl.gov.uk
Rail:
London Charing Cross, London Bridge, Abbey Wood, Dartford
www.southeasternrailway.co.uk
Water Bus
Thames Clipper to Greenwich
www.thamesclippers.com

Parking: Best to use public transport
Greenwich: Pay and Display
Abbey Wood: Pay and Display
Lesnes Abbey: On Street

Accommodation:
London, Greenwich, Rochester
Use any as a base and connect by train
Appendix 4: Tourist Information links
Caravan Club: Abbey Park ½ mile

Refreshments: See Appendix 3
Greenwich: Many and varied
Thames Barrier: Terrace Café:
Thursday to Sunday 10.30 to 5pm
Marryon Park: Café and toilets

Plumstead Common: Small supermarkets, shops
Lesnes Abbey: None
Abbey Wood: The Abbey Arms
Small supermarkets, shops

Connecting Long Distance Paths:
Jubilee Greenway
The Thames Path National Trail
Green Chain Walk

Geography
The first stage to the Thames Barrier is alongside the River Thames. The landscape changes as we leave the Thames and follow the Green Chain Walk. The first climb is 167ft to Woolwich Common, a steep descent and an ascent to Bostall Woods, 217ft followed by undulating paths through the Lesnes Abbey Woods. The parks and open spaces are amazing and such variation in the scenery was not expected. It is a pity that there are no outstanding views of the City.

Path Profile & Difficulty
Flat and then hilly.
Moderate effort on the steepish climbs.
Footpaths are well defined with the occasional kissing gate and mostly waymarked. The Thames Path's hard and unrelenting surface can be tiring. An added difficulty is the lack of refreshment and toilet facilities along this section.

Reflections

From the magnificence of Greenwich to the iconic steel hoods of the Thames Barrier shining in the sunlight, a broad walkway allows you to stroll next to a much wider river than before. Working wharves line the riverside giving an industrial air to the area and the occasional decaying pier or warehouse only serves as a reminder that London was once the busiest port in the world. Ships moored all along The Thames up to London Bridge, all the hustle and bustle of cargos from all around the world being unloaded, helping an older London expand to meet new needs. The wharves now lie mostly idle, larger ships need deeper water and the Port has moved to Tilbury, further down the river, but there is still the feeling of a history. Away from the river, there are parks and ancient woodland that have survived for a thousand years, a world distant from the streets of London. So beautiful are the trees and trails, and the solitude and inspiration they provide, that it is hard to imagine how close you are to the City.

The Walk

Leaving Greenwich Station at 10.15 on a bright and warm Saturday morning in April I turned left to walk down Greenwich High Road towards the River and past the Cutty Sark

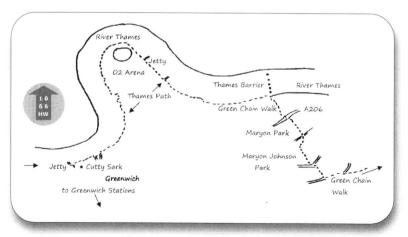

The Saxon Times

Rochester   11th October 1066

Today with the Kings Army

From your War Correspondent

Today, King Harold and the main force of the English army marched out of London. They crossed London Bridge and headed off down the Dover road towards Crayford without waiting for the expected reinforcements.

New recruits raised in the Home Counties were expected to arrive later today, but Harold has sent messengers telling them to assemble "at the Hoar Apple-Tree".

This is a well-known landmark at the junction of the Sussex Hundreds of Baldstow, Hailesaltede and Ninfield.

The tree stands on Caldbec Hill, where the road leading north from Hastings forks. One branch leads to the road that runs from Maidstone to London, the other to the Lewes-London road.

I believe that the Army will cross the River Medway tonight, over what is left of the old bridge, much repaired since the Romans left. Communication is scarce especially amongst the lower ranks – they just follow the horses of their leaders without question.

As the Army progresses along Watling Street they are joined by local recruits and conscripts from nearby manors. The new soldiers, many of whom have never fought in anger before, show an unease hidden behind   nervous laughter.

Their disposition is not helped by the stories of blood and battle from the regular soldiers who push them all along at speed to ensure that they make camp by sunset. They have to watch their step as well, there are holes in the road deep enough to break a leg, mud like glue and deep ditches either side.

Some of the older soldiers run off the main track and come back with small birds or animals in their hands, some with vegetables or fruit and I even saw one with a deer, all stolen in the name of the King, and all destined for the pot.

By nightfall, the camp is set, fires lit and there is a smell of cooking in the air. Snatches of music and singing can be heard, a fight breaks out but is soon stopped and an uneasy peace descends.

Tomorrow, the same march again to reach the Appledore Estuary, at Bodiam, and then just a short march to Caldbec Hill and the junction of the old ridge roads.

As Earl of Wessex, Harold knows this part of England well. The terrain is hilly and far from ideal for the cavalry that, rumour has it, makes up much of the Norman forces.

If Harold can hold Caldbec Hill, the Norman forces will be bottled up in Hastings and William will find it difficult to resupply his army during the winter.

Long Live the King.

resplendent in its new surroundings (in 2010, it was wrapped in polythene after the depressing fire in May 2007). Opposite Greenwich Pier is The Isle of Dogs and Docklands with Canary Wharf watching over London.

Turn right along the river in front of the impressive Greenwich University, formerly the old Greenwich Naval College and at the end of the path is the Trafalgar Tavern – whitebait restaurant and haunt of the famous and infamous since the 18th century.

Turn right and then left, following the Thames Path past The Yacht and continue to re-join the river where there are marker stones set in the wall to identify the high water levels of 1874 and 1928. On the right is the resplendent Trinity Hospital, dwarfed by the power station looming darkly to one side.

The Cutty Sark Tavern, 1795, and a sign board on Ballast Quay gives some of the history of the quay. It is too early to stop but if you are staying the night in Greenwich it could be an evening stroll away from The Trafalgar and The Yacht. There are benches here to take the evening air and a pint.

The 'shining' Thames Barrier

The O2 Arena

The Thames Path has now re-opened almost in its entirety after the 2012 Olympics. The memory of a landscape laid waste, the noise, dust, path closures, pointless diversions and the lack of proper information will all be forgotten and once again I can enjoy walking by the riverside albeit with a very different skyline.

This industrial South Bank is losing its history, identity and industry in favour of flats and apartments and a new 'prosperity' beginning with the 2012 Olympics and this section of the Thames Path will appear very different in future. Factory walls and chimneys have been demolished opening up the view towards our immediate destination, the O2 Arena or 'Millennium Dome', built to celebrate the dawn of a new millennium.

At Ballast Key, continue up the ramp in front of the now completed Lovell's Wharf development.

There are beaches down by the river with a medley of plastic and wood washed up by the tide, barges and lighters left to perish, working wharves and wooden jetties left to rot, new factories with gleaming steel and glass and demolition sites levelled for progress. We must hope that there is some grand design for the future that will complement the river and

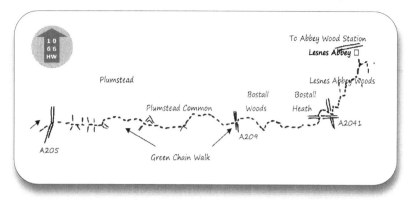

preserve the Thames Path. In places the path is lined by surreal willow trees, as if by some rural stream, that hide Canary Wharf from view.

Once past Victoria Deep Water Terminal the O2 Arena dominates the river. In 2012, the terminal was alive with earth movers of all shapes and sizes – a portrayal of some eternal enterprise that is forever destined to move earth, a giant Tonka toy playground.

With the Thames Path fully restored, you can reflect on the remnants of past glories with the tracks for the cranes still in evidence and opposite, on the North Bank, the entrance to West India Dock. From the O2 Arena to the Thames Barrier, The Thames Path is well signposted with story boards along the way, the first advising that we are at the Victoria Deep Water Terminal and next is a post that celebrates the Greenwich Meridian and two miles to the Thames Barrier.

At the Greenwich Yacht Club turn right and then left and follow the path to re-join the river. It is ten miles from Tower Bridge and this walk has still never really left the Docks. It must have been some sight when all the wharves were lined with cargo ships from around the world – noisy, smelly, busy, alive. Leave the river again, past more sites devoted to providing resources for regeneration and development, but this was always an industrial landscape so why should it offend now?

In Saxon times, the muddy creeks that can still be seen would have been used to beach boats for unloading and a further 9 miles downstream by boat, was Erith (pronounced Ear-ith) from the Saxon meaning 'gravelly landing place or muddy harbour' ('The Place Names of Kent', Judith Glover).

Half a mile from the Thames Barrier, we pass The Hope and Anchor with seats and benches by the Thames. Soon there are photo opportunities, refreshments and toilets before we leave the Thames and head inland using the Green Chain Walk (GCW). The Terrace Café is just the other side of the Barrier, along a subway with a mural depicting the drop in the Thames from the source to the sea.

At the Barrier, turn right and follow the signs to Maryon Park, first along the road and then to meander along the green trail which brings you to the main road and a Pelican Crossing. Enter the Park and turn left to follow the signs to 'Charlton Parks and Oxleas Wood: 4 miles'.

Up the rise with the playground on the right, bear right and continue with the tennis courts on the left until the GCW points up the steps to the right. The steps are a rude awakening after the flat of the Thames Path and herald more climbs ahead. Continue up the hill, through the gate at the top, bear right along the path and cross the road to continue the GCW into Maryon Wilson Park. Take the path through the middle of the animal farm, turn left and follow the GCW signs up the hill, towards Charlton Park. The wildness here is far removed from the industrial Thames and is a feature of the GCW with more to come.

Leave the park, cross the road, turn right and almost immediately left to follow the footpath fingerpost into Charlton Park. Continue along the path as it bends to the left into Cemetery Lane and turn right. At the junction turn left into Charlton Park Lane which becomes Ha Ha Road then Barrack Park and which leads into Nightingale Place, Edge Hill and Plumstead Common Road.

At the traffic lights, we have climbed 167ft from the Thames but there are higher points to come. The Barracks of The Royal

Artillery can be seen on the other side of the Barrack Park.

Follow the GCW for 1½ miles to reach The Prince of Wales pub (now closed 2011), turn left and follow the GCW posts into the Common and continue straight ahead. Cross Blendon Terrace following the path up the rise past the tennis courts and across the small park to bear left at The Old Mill pub (with the remnants of the old mill behind), into the aptly named Old Mill Road. Enter the Common and keep to the railings on the left. The path is clearly marked down and up steps to bear left at the top, around the playground, and follow the GCW signs to 'Bostall Woods'.

Down and up, across Winn Lane, through the gap in the railings and head east towards the GCW signpost on the other side of Winn's Common. Pick up the path down through the woods to Wickham Lane, cross and enter Bostall Woods at the GCW sign in Rutherglen Road.

Climb the steepish hill ahead and follow the GCW signs up until, at 240ft, we reach the high point of this section of 1066 Harold's Way.

We are surrounded by broad leaved trees and regrettably there are no views of London but the tracks that we follow may be reminiscent of the forests of Andreasweald, a 1000 years ago – imagination is a wonderful thing and takes the mind off the labours of 1066 Harold's Way under a hot sun.

The path opens up into a clearing with picnic tables. We have covered around 8½ miles and there is only the final descent left to Lesnes Abbey, 1¼ miles away. Round the bowling green, turn left to cross Longleigh Lane and follow the GCW signs around the edge of Bostall Heath, across Bostall Hill Road and down the path into the woods. Turn right along the track. Cross the road and follow the GCW signs through a small complex of flats to the end of the road and turn right. A little way along the road is the entrance to the woods on your left.

As we follow the GCW down through the woods you can forget that you are still in London. The broad leaved trees do give the impression that you are walking along some ancient trackway similar to the tracks that Harold may have followed. It is a world away from today's Watling Street to the south, for which we should be thankful. I know that it is not following the exact footsteps of Harold but this is an altogether much more delightful route.

Follow the GCW down the hill and turn right towards the small pond. Continue down the hill, bearing left, cross the road and just when you looked up and thought that you had to climb the hill in front, turn left, leaving the GCW, to follow the path down the hill to the Abbey ruins at the bottom. The gardens are beautifully kept and the ruins well maintained and they still give off an air of solitude. Head for the Information Office where there are toilets, but no refreshments, and the sound of a distant ice cream van is almost too much to bear.

Lesnes Abbey is a fitting end to this walk and reflects the change from industrial to rural, city to suburban and river to hills. There is much more open landscape to come for the remainder of 1066 Harold's Way.

For Abbey Wood Station, ¼ mile away, cross the footbridge ahead, down the steps into Abbey Road and turn right heading towards and under the flyover ahead. Turn right and the station is in front with the Abbey Arms opposite.

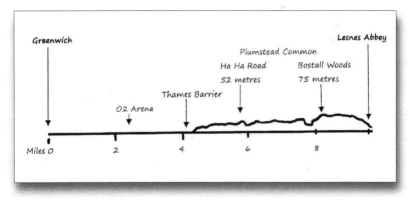

43

Isle of Dogs. www.islandhistory.org.uk/

Trinity Hospital Greenwich. This magnificent decorated building dates back to 1613 and is the oldest surviving building in Greenwich town centre.
http://www.mercers.co.uk/downloads/TRINITY_HOSPITAL_GREENWICH_-_HH.pdf

O2 Arena. Originally christened 'The Dome', it was constructed to celebrate the third Millenium and housed the Millennium Experience exhibition. Now named 'The O2.Arena', it has become a major music venue with a cinema, exhibition space, piazzas and bars and restaurants.

Thames Barrier. This is the major flood control for the River Thames and London. Built between 1974 and 1982 it was first used defensively in 1983. The silver pods house the hydraulic machinery needed to raise the 10 movable steel gates during periods of tidal surge. It is the world's second largest movable flood barrier, the largest is the Maeslantkering in The Netherlands.
http://www.environment-agency.gov.uk/homeandleisure/floods/38353.aspx

Maryon Park was once the site of a Roman hill fort and Cox's Mount, the highest point, was used as a bearing to adjust ships' compasses.

Maryon Wilson Park was part of the Hanging Wood and originally a hideaway for the highwaymen of Shooters Hill and Blackheath. The animal park provides a welcome contrast to the Thames Path.

Charlton, Woolwich and Plumstead. This was all farm land and orchards in Saxon times. There is also a connection with Harold. Earl Godwin took the plum orchards of Plumstede from St Augustine's Abbey to give to his brother, Tostig, before King Edward re-possessed them. After Edward's death, Tostig seized them again until he was exiled by Harold.

Bostall Woods. Bostall comes from the OE, a place of refuge, and it still has a beauty and a solitude with which to enjoy the climb through the woodland of broad leafed trees.

Lesnes Abbey Woods. The Abbey was built on meadowland beside the river in 1178. Despite the idyllic setting the monks fought a losing battle to maintain the river banks and drain the marsh and it was already falling into disrepair in the 14th century. Now, in May, the woods beside the Abbey are famous for their wild daffodils and bluebells.
http://www.bexley.gov.uk/index.aspx?articleid=3906

1066 HAROLD'S WAY WALK 3:
LESNES ABBEY TO
DARTFORD ⟨🚶 Public Footpath⟩

Distance: 9.75 miles
Time: 3½ hours
Maps: OS Explorer 162
        London A-Z
        www.streetmap.co.uk
        (for Abbey Wood / Dartford)

Travel:
www.travelinesoutheast.org.uk
www.nationalrail.co.uk
Rail:
London Bridge, Abbey Wood, Dartford,
www.southeasternrailway.co.uk

Parking
Abbey Wood: Pay and Display
Lesnes Abbey: On Street
Dartford: Pay and Display

For Lesnes Abbey, follow the waymarks for
the Green Chain Walk from Abbey Wood
Station and cross the footbridge that leads
directly into the Park. Allow 10 minutes.

Accommodation
London, Greenwich and Rochester
Use any as a base and connect by train and
bus
Caravan Club: Abbey Park ½ mile
Appendix 4: Tourist Information links

Refreshments
Abbey Wood: Small supermarkets, shops
Lesnes Abbey: None
Erith Various shops and pubs and a large
supermarket

Dartford The Stage Door (Shepherds Neame),
B&B. Major shopping centre with everything
you would need
Connecting Long Distance Paths
Thames Path: www.thames-path.org.uk
Green Chain Walk: www.greenchain.com
London Loop: www.walklondon.org.uk
Darent Valley Walk:
www.kent.gov.uk/explorekent

Geography
The parkland and broad leaved woods of
Lesnes Abbey lead into the streets of
Belvedere, Franks Park and finally to the Erith
Riverside. The industrial zone that follows is
less than inspiring but persevere and enjoy the
flood banks of the Thames, Dartford Creek,
the River Cray and the River Darent into
Dartford.

Path Profile & Difficulty Hilly and then flat
– moderate to easy.
The undulating paths through the Lesnes
Abbey Woods rise to 200ft but there is an
easy descent to regain the Thames Path into
Erith. The remainder is a river walk and flat.
There are just two stiles and the occasional
kissing gate.
This walk follows the Green Chain Walk and
Thames Path to Erith and the London Loop to
Dartford. Footpaths are well defined and
mostly waymarked as they all relate to
established trails. However, there are
occasions when the signs are not clear.

Reflections

This is a mixture of the wild and desolate and the urban and industrial, of old paths and new roads, old bridges and new bridges, meandering rivers and canals built in hope, Saxon Manors and concrete architecture. We pass the detritus of modern urban and industrial re-development and the solitude of a Church that figured in history during King John's reign.

It is a walk that reflects the dreams of men and often their failure, from the monks of Lesnes Abbey who fought to hold back the Thames to the navigators and entrepreneurs of Dartford, building a ship canal that could not cope with the pressure of the tide.

The Walk

If you are early or not in a rush, Lesnes Abbey is worth a wander around the ruins and well kept gardens reading the storyboards – if the sun is shining it is a peaceful and relaxed start to a walk.

Start at the Lesnes Abbey Information Office, facing the ruined nave turn right and follow the path and waymarks round to a gap in the hedge. Bear left into the trees and follow the GCW signposted to 'Franks Park and Erith Riverside 2½ miles', about an hour away as there are hills to climb. In spring, these woods are renowned for being carpeted with wild flowers.

A small ascent to start, after ten minutes left and right, but soon it is a decent climb to 194 feet (60 metres) – a more than

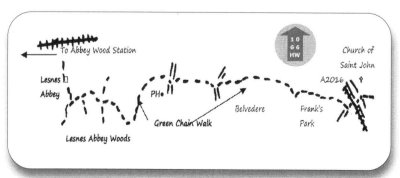

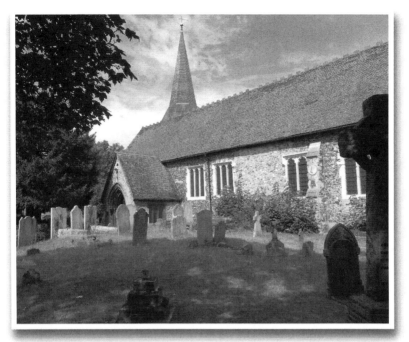

The Church of St John, Erith

undulating start and perhaps a 6 or 7 in terms of effort but safe in the knowledge that it is the only climb. Follow the GCW and at the bottom of the hill, turn right along a track (Leather Bottle Lane) and right into St Augustine's Road. Continue up the hill to The Leather Bottle PH and turn left into Upper Abbey Road following the GCW - it is waymarked.

Cross Picardy Road into Holt Robin Road and head down to the entrance into Franks Park on the right - it is now a mile to Erith Riverside. Follow the GCW past the children's playground (which looks great fun) and bear left. Leave the park and at the end of Valley Road turn left to cross the railway footbridge and the old Parish Church of St John the Baptist, Erith appears in front. The church's history is said to include events that occurred after King John signed the Magna Carta in 1215, 150 years on from the Battle of Hastings.

47

Mud, looking down river at Erith

After the church, bear left and continue the GCW towards the river along Corinthian Manor Way and turn right towards Erith. This is a very different Thames to the one that we left at the Thames Barrier – mud flats and wide open spaces and the Queen Elizabeth II Bridge dominates in the distance. A mile to go to Erith.

Keep to the lower walkway and at the William Cory Promenade there are signs for the Station and Riverside Gardens, Thames Path and the London Loop. Crayford Ness is 2¼ miles away.

There are views of the busy river from the Gardens, tugs and lighters, small boats and bigger cargo ships can all pass before you. Look back up river and there is little to see of London and on my grey day there was just a wide expanse of mud and an equally grey river. Down river, 1066 Harold's Way will pass by the beacons of Crayford Ness framed by the Q E Bridge. Follow the signs towards the Town Centre, Thames Path and the Deep Water Jetty. Turn left into an alley between the Cross Keys (now closed) and The Playhouse, the path loops behind the Cross Keys, down to the river to follow the waymarks towards Wharfside Close and a storyboard detailing some of Erith's history. After the Pier, bear left to re-join the river and at the end of the walkway, turn right to follow the road and waymarks behind Morrison's, into Apollo Road and left along Manor Road. Industry prevents us walking along the river bank and this is the start of a half mile slog between the railings and

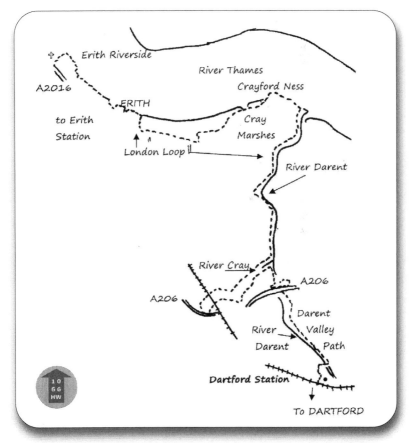

gates of depots and vacant lots. The noise and dust of this industrial wasteland provides a stark contrast to the sudden calm and wilderness of the Marshes.

Follow the signs to Erith Yacht Club and continue along the path, on the top of the flood bank, to Crayford Ness now just a mile away.

For me, the wind blew across the Marsh and rain could be felt in the wind. The Thames wound its way towards the QE Bridge

---

The Saxon Times

Rochester	Late Edition	11th October 1066

Today with the Saxon Army

From your War Correspondent embedded with the Saxon Army

It has been a tough few days for our men, but they remain in good spirits.

The core of the Army has increased with local recruitment and there is a spirit of victory in the air following the battles in the North.

We made good speed along the old Roman Road from the Capital.

The camp fires have been lit, shelter provided and animals slaughtered.

As with all armies, once we have been fed, there is the singing of old songs and the telling of tales of battles long ago, of Hengest and Horsa and the beginnings of our Saxon Kingdom.

We Saxons feel at home here for Kent is in our blood.

Warning.

There have been reports of Norman spies being seen in the area.

We have all been asked to be vigilant, even you the public.

If you see anybody acting suspiciously inform your village elder.

Remember, careless talk costs lives.

We have seen little of King Harold II.

The King is mostly in meetings with his brothers, Gyrth and Leofwine, and his *housecarls* but there is word that he will take time, later tonight, to ride around the camp.

A final note.

You can rest assured that the Saxon Army is well trained and battle hardened.

Our fearsome axes still bear the blood of beaten Vikings

Our shield wall will stand firm against the Norman arrows.

The invaders will be repelled.

We march tomorrow towards the 'Old Hoar Apple Tree'.

Long Live King Harold II.

The Green Man that
protects Lesnes Abbey
Woods and helps
walkers on their way

that dwarfs the chimney of the Littlebrook Power Station and
the Crayford Ness beacons. The tide is out, the River Darent
almost dry and the dark grey sculpture of the Flood Defence
adds to the desolation. Ignore the breakers yards behind and
read the story boards.

Keep to the path beside the River Darent and bear left to
reach the River Cray. With water levels as they are there is little
evidence of how navigable the river must have been in the 19th
century. Ahead is the road bridge that we need to cross to join
the Darent Valley Path into Dartford.

Follow the River Cray into the industrial estate, where the
starlings perched on the radio mast provide a cacophony of
sound that challenges the machines working in the
neighbouring yards. Under the railway bridge and bear left to

A defence against the dark arts, a brooding cathedral of the marsh, but in reality a flood defence gate on a marsh creek.

Barnes Cray and then left again at the main road, the A206 signposted to the M25.

Over the River Cray and turn left at the Public Footpath 249 sign to follow the path on the other side of the Cray. Continue along the flood bank round to the A206 and turn left, cross the road bridge and follow the path left back underneath the dual carriageway, to join the Darent Valley Path towards Dartford.

The locks and the weir have fallen into disrepair and are now just a poignant reminder of a previous prosperity but there are plans to redevelop the waterfront and canal and in future years there may be a very different landscape. There is already a new path that takes you to the footbridge over the river into Lower Hythe Street.

So many of the old factories and mills have been demolished that you wonder what will appear in its place but it should not change the river walk or our route to Central Park.

Turn left past the Hufflers Arms to the island, keep left, cross Mill Pond Road and follow the road signs to the station, under the railway bridge. The station is up the steps to the left but, for a quiet pint for a weary traveller, The Stage Door (SN) is just five minutes way along Hythe Street.

If you need to sample the delights of Dartford, for food or drink, the following directions are taken from the beginning of the next walk:

Continue along Mill Pond Road, past the station perched high above, to a break in the wall and join the river walk to the Town Centre. There is water in the river and although sometimes choked with reeds it provides living and sleeping accommodation for a variety of ducks and further on are grape vines and grapes – Chateau Dartford perhaps, but the Romans were probably there first with their own Pinot Grigio.

As the buildings end, turn right and follow the waymarks into the underpass below the busy ring road. Turn left through the gardens towards Holy Trinity Church and into the High Street that follows the line of the old Roman Road. The history of Dartford is told on the many story boards in the town and although they may delay you a little they are well worth the read. There are pubs, delis, cafes and supermarkets in Dartford to meet all kinds of lunch time requirements - my hot salt beef sandwich on brown bread was particularly good.

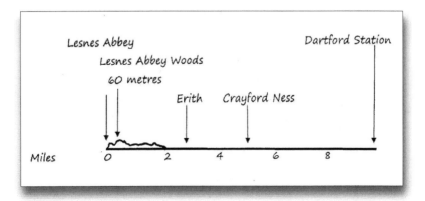

The Church of St John

This church has Saxon arches by the altar and a history, for it is rumored that in 1215, the Barons held assembly here to settle the civil war that followed the signing of the Magna Carta. www.kentchurches.info/church.asp?p=Erith+1

Erith

Saxon in origin, Erith meaning 'muddy harbour' or 'gravelly landing place' and it was once one of the great shipyards of the Thames. Erith was a port in Saxon times and later, after Henry VIII's decision to open a naval dockyard, it built the Great Harry, the ship that took the King of England in all his glory to the Field of the Cloth of Gold in France. It was the biggest ship of the time. Until the 1850s, Erith continued as a small riverside port and a popular anchorage. Ships often discharged part of their cargo at Erith, lightening their load before sailing upstream through the shallows. In the 1960s, much of Old Erith was redeveloped into 'a modern, sleek shopping and working environment' and all that remains of the old town are Queens Church, The Cross Keys pub and the 19th century Christ Church.

Crayford

At Crayford, where the River Cray joins the Darent and then the Thames, the remains of a woolly rhinoceros were found, surrounded by the Stone Age weapons of the men who had killed it, and one of the finest skulls of a great caved lion found in England. A little way up stream, where Watling Street crosses the river, the Battle of Cregan-ford was fought in 457 ending in defeat for the Britons (four thousand slaughtered) and further established Hengest as the first Saxon king of Kent, a dynasty that would last for 600 years to 1066.

Dartford

'The ford over the River Darent' became established as a major river crossing-point and was a focal point between two Roman routes - that from west to east, part of the main route connecting London and the Continent and to the south following the Darent valley. There is evidence of Roman and Saxon occupation and the Roman Watling Street divides the modern town. William certainly came through Dartford after the Battle of Hastings had been won. Later, it became a traveller's rest for pilgrims on their way to Canterbury and our path, 1066 Harold's Way, lies south along the Darent River, through Central Park.

On the approach into Dartford, before the Darent runs under the main street, there was a bend in the river that would have created a little harbour. In the 1830s, fifty years before the Manchester Ship Canal, a project was started to canalise the river to create a small inland port allowing Dartford's engineering industry access the Thames and to overseas. The weir and the lock that are passed were part of this grand scheme but both are now in need of some repair.

1066 HAROLD'S WAY WALK 4:
DARTFORD TO
ISTEAD RISE

Distance: 9.25 miles
Time: 3½ hours
Maps: OS Explorer 162
Beacon Wood Country Park
http://www.users.waitrose.com/ ~ beanra/par
k-bigmap.html

Travel: www.travelinesoutheast.org.uk
www.nationalrail.co.uk
Rail:
London Charing Cross, London Bridge,
Dartford, Gravesend, Meopham
www.southeasternrailway.co.uk
Bus
Arriva Kent Thameside 306/308:
Istead Rise Gravesend/Istead Rise Meopham
Taxi - local
Meopham, Station Approach
Parking
Dartford: Pay and Display
Istead Rise: Car Park & On Street

Accommodation:
London, Greenwich, Rochester
Use any as a base and connect by train
Appendix 4: Tourist Information links
Bean: Black Horse Cottage B&B

Refreshments:
Dartford: Many and varied
Darenth: The Chequers
Bean: Black Horse
Village shop

Southfleet: The Ship
Food served every day
12.00 to 2.30 and all day Sunday to 6.30.
Istead Rise: Co-operative Supermarket
Village Bakers
Meopham: Railway Inn
Gravesend: The Grapes SN
Crown & Thistle
(Good Beer Guide)

Connecting Long Distance Paths:
Darent Valley Walk

Geography
Undulating
Leave Dartford through Central Park and
follow the River Darent before climbing onto
the chalk downs. The rest of the walk is
mostly across fields, woods and Beacon
Wood Country Park.

Path Profile & Difficulty
Reasonably easy section with just one
moderate climb.
Flat river walk to Darenth followed by a climb
for 1¼ miles to Lords Wood, a rise of 328ft
from sea level. The remaining walk is
undulating and varies between 150 and
300ft. There is only a little road walking but
there are footpaths and along the country
lanes traffic is minimal. Medium effort, some
stiles but footpaths on the whole well
defined.

Reflections

Crossing Watling Street, now Dartford's High Street, we can say our goodbyes to London. Away from the River Darent, 1066 Harold's Way climbs up to give a first taste of the North Downs and the beautiful views south over the Darent Valley and west along the line of the Downs towards Surrey. There is just the hint of a hidden population amidst the rolling hills and valleys, lush fields and rows of trees as far as the eye can see. The noise of the traffic gives way to the solitude of a church built from the rubble of a Roman villa 1000 years ago. It stood as Harold passed. This is old Saxon land that we are walking on and he would have drawn support here and on the rest of the march for his important battle ahead.

Grassland, paddocks, fields of crops, woods, country parks, the occasional farm and villages that were once prosperous but seem to have now lost their heart, with the closure of pub, post office and shop. Their character still remains, from the quarry houses of Bean to the 'crinkle crankle' wall at Betsham. Southfleet is different. It is old with a long history and equally important an old pub, 'The Ship', to savour 1066 Harold's Way.

The Walk

Leave Dartford Station and walk west past the small curved parade of shops and down the steps to the right. At the bottom turn right and right again along Mill Pond Road. At the break in the wall, join the River Walk to the Town Centre. There is water in the river and although sometimes choked with reeds it provides living and sleeping accommodation for a variety of ducks. A little further on are grape vines and grapes – Chateau Dartford perhaps, but the Romans were probably there first with their own Pinot Grigio.

As the buildings end, turn right and follow the waymarks into the underpass below the busy ring road, waymarked Darent Valley Path. Turn left through the gardens towards Holy Trinity Church and turn right into the High Street that follows the line of the old Roman Road. The many story boards give a history

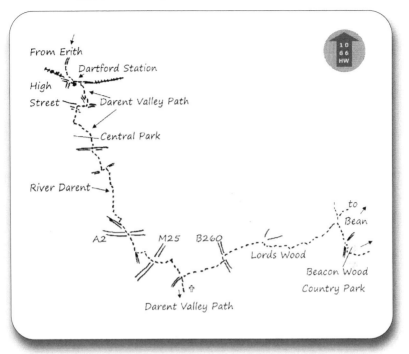

of Dartford and one includes the suggestion that the birthplace of Wat Tyler, now the Wat Tyler Arms, was built some time after his death!

Continue along High Street and turn left into Market Place following the signs for the Library and Central Park. Into the Park and walk straight ahead towards the bandstand. At the bandstand turn left and follow the signs for the Darent Valley Path, past the playground and the Café in the Park, to the river. Bear right, past the Skate Board Park and the running track into the tunnel under Princes Road. At the lake take the middle path, straight ahead, that skirts the lake and exit into Powder Mill Lane. Turn left, cross the bridge and take the waymarked footpath right.

This is a very English walk by a meandering river through the dappled shade of the trees and a world away from our industrial heritage and the windswept Cray Marshes. Follow

Reflections, Central Park Dartford

the path, for about ten minutes, to the footbridge over the river and continue into Hawley Lane. Turn left, under the A2 flyover and walk towards Hawley taking the footpath, opposite Mill Road, back to the River Darent and under the M25 Motorway. September would be a good month to pick the blackberries by the side of the path - unless somebody got there before you.

After the M25, follow the waymarks, left, across the field to enter Darenth Road to the left of the house in front. Past The Chequers PH and turn left to walk up Darenth Hill. On the right set back from the road is St Margaret's Church with its Saxon and Norman history, partly built from Roman stone looted from the local villa, and at the top of the hill is the aptly named Roman Villa Road. At the T junction in Darenth, turn left, cross the road and turn right up Wood Lane, by the Fox and Hounds pub (closed).

Wood Lane continues into a footpath and climbs up to 100 metres (330 feet). As the path levels out at the metalled road, that curves around in front like a letter 'V', turn right into the wood and immediately take the path on the left through the trees. This woodland track weaves and turns, dappled sunshine lighting the way and in spring, bluebells give colour. Into the open, surprised by the commanding views south and west, I take a few minutes before looking left towards Lords Wood. Head across the field to a point about 60 metres to the right of the top corner, and follow the path through Lords Wood. Back into the open and continue the path by the side of the trees that will soon reveal Bean Farm nestling in the valley below. Roman Watling Street, and Harold's route to Rochester, lies parallel to the north but it now resounds to the army of motorway travellers providing a backdrop to the birdsong of Lords Wood.

Close to Bean Farm, turn right along the waymarked path, over the stile and into Shellbank Lane, the stile to enter Beacon Wood Country Park is opposite to the right. Over the stile and turn immediately right to follow the path round to the brick building (Bore Hole D, Western Beacon Wood, Thames Water

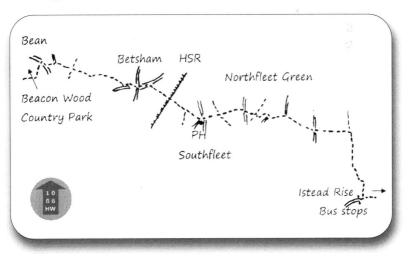

The Saxon Times

Hastings   12th October 1066

Inside the enemy camp.

From our undercover reporter

Hastings is not a good place for a Saxon to be at this time. The church has been under the control of the Bishop of Fecamp for many years and there is much anti-Saxon feeling. The soldiers have the same bloodlust as their Viking forefathers and I have seen the results first hand when they sacked Bexhill.

Norman intelligence has reported that the English army is on its way from London.

They are marching down the Dover Road and have crossed the Medway at Rochester.

There is a belief that in Harold's haste, some of the army may have been left behind to recover from the long march from York. They will follow on later.

William, Duke of Normandy, and his Council of War are delighted.

By contrast, William's army seem well rested in their long established safe haven, at Hastings, and are ready for a fight.

They had been dreading a long, drawn-out campaign and believe a swift engagement will be to their advantage.

The Norman army is getting ready to move from the security of Hastings and Hastings Castle to a new camp on Telham Hill, five miles to the north.

My informants tell me of Duke William's intention to meet Harold's army close to the crossroads at Senlac Hill.

Sources close to the Duke admit that these strategic crossroads hold the key to the invasion.

Win here and **William** could be crowned King by Christmas.

I fear for England and our Saxon Rights and our Rule of Law.

We must not submit to Norman dictatorship.

It will not be benevolent.

We will be forced from our lands.

Our lives will be controlled by fear and uncertainty.

Taxation will destroy our way of life.

French will become our language.

It is not the future that we want for our sons

Trust me.

Long Live King Harold II

River Darent

Bore Hole) turn left to join one of the main paths, south-east through the wood.

All the paths are well laid through this mixed wood with silver birch and oak and relics of the quarry's past. Dog walkers and strollers and couples hand in hand bring life to this beautiful park rescued from waste, true recycling, but there are many divergent paths - just keep straight ahead. When the main path, the blue route, bears right down past the picnic tables towards the car park we turn left and after about 70 metres, take the right hand fork, up the steps and leave the park. Into School Lane, opposite and to the right, and as School Lane bears left take the clear waymarked footpath in the corner towards Betsham.

As the path descends, look ahead towards the horizon and if the weather is clear Istead Rise can be seen, marked out by its size. At Betsham Road, turn left to the crossroads and the now defunct Collyers Arms (replaced by housing). Into Station Road, signposted to Northfleet and Gravesend, and after about a 100 metres there is the waymarked footpath on the right through an opening in the grand brick wall (Kent CC path 29). Spend a second to look a little further along Station Road as adjacent to the footpath is a fine example of a 'Crinkle Crankle Wall', built curving and snake-like to add strength and support. The path leads to Southfleet, under the high speed train line and Southfleet Church appears in front. There are timber framed houses and the old Ship Inn. The Sedley Trust School is on the corner and the bus, Arriva 439, calls three times a day. It is a place to let time rush by on its own, a pint and lunch before the final section to Istead Rise, two miles away for there is little at Istead Rise but houses and a parade of shops.

Towards Betsham

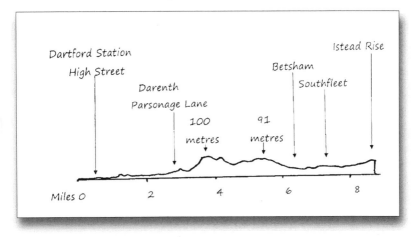

Into Warren Road, and at Scadbury Manor (part late 17th century), take the waymarked footpath to the right of the barn opposite and on to Northfleet Green Road, turn left and as the road turns left again, follow the waymarked path straight ahead, parallel with Watling Street. The clear path continues east towards the veritable forest of pylons from the power stations by the Thames – we will use them as markers.

Through the kissing gates and head towards the second pylon, down steps and continue straight ahead across the middle of the second field. Up the steps, across Downs Road and follow the path straight ahead into the second field and in the middle of the field (TQ634709), in line with the second pylon, turn right along the track towards Istead Rise. Continue south through the woods, past the sports ground on the left, into Worcester Close and finally left into the village centre with its car park, shops and bus stops.

The bus connects to the stations at Gravesend and Meopham with their links to London and Rochester. There is the Railway Inn at Meopham but Gravesend has more to offer with its shopping centre and a few pubs that come well recommended and are well worth a visit. Both Gravesend and Meopham are around 10 minutes away by bus.

Darenth

The Darent River was what appeared to be a 'property hotspot' for Roman villas two thousand years ago and the remains of one can be visited at Lullingstone (EH) further upriver. The great Roman house that stood at Darenth was over 400ft long and nearly as wide and furnished with every current luxury of the time. Sadly there is little of the Roman to see now but it is likely that the stone, tiles and brickwork would have been used by the Saxons to build the church. The Normans left their own mark and with later additions in the English style the church became how it appears today.

Just up the hill from Darenth Road is a little green and through an avenue of chestnuts we can see the church, shaded by an old yew tree, it depends on your time whether you visit the church.

Lords Wood is named after William Lord, circa 1400, a local landowner.

Beacon Wood Country Park has a varied and interesting history. Relics of the site's industrial past can still be seen in the foundation blocks of gunpowder buildings, gravel heaps from clay washing and the routes of the railway lines used to transport clay. The work left beds of sandstone and sandy clays with the middle areas of rock made up almost entirely of shells and fossils and sharks' teeth have been found from a time long ago when this was water.

Park map: http://www.users.waitrose.com/ ~ beanra/park-bigmap.html
Information:
http://www.users.waitrose.com/ ~ beanra/countrypark.html

Betsham

Crinkle Crankle Walls
http://www.history.org.uk/resources/general_resource_2534_74.html

Southfleet

The history of Southfleet can be traced back to Roman and Saxon times. Then, it sat close to the River Fleet and there is some evidence of a Roman dock. These navigable rivers must have been the lifeblood for such communities although the river is some way away now. Watling Street runs close enough to the north to justify the path of 1066 Harold's Way. The Ship Inn is old and worth a visit.

http://www.britishlistedbuildings.co.uk/en-172690-the-ship-inn-southfleet
Southfleet was also the home of Sir John Sedley a landowner and benefactor. In 1637, he founded the local school in Southfleet. I was once a Trustee for the Sir John Sedley Trust in Wymondham, near Melton Mowbray where, under the terms of his will, his widow Elizabeth invested £400 to support a Schoolmaster to teach the children of the village. Lady Elizabeth died in Wymondham in 1649 but was buried in Kent. ('The Sir John Sedley Charity' by Ralph Penniston-Taylor)

Scadbury Manor

http://www.britishlistedbuildings.co.uk/en-172675-scadbury-manor-southfleet
Istead Rise http://www.discovergravesham.co.uk/istead-rise/istead-rise-settlement-development.html

1066 HAROLD'S WAY WALK 5:
ISTEAD RISE TO ROCHESTER ⟨🚶 Public Footpath⟩

Distance: 8.75 miles
Time: 3 hours
Maps: OS Explorer: 148 & 162

Travel
www.travelinesoutheast.org.uk

Rail:
South Eastern:
Charing Cross/London Bridge to Gravesend,
Strood, Rochester
www.southeasternrailway.co.uk
Bus
Arriva Kent Thameside 306/308:
Gravesend to Istead Rise
Meopham to Istead Rise
Taxi
Meopham Station Approach

Parking
Istead Rise: Car Park & On Street
Jeskyns Country Park: Car park
Strood & Rochester: Pay and Display

Accommodation
London, Greenwich and Rochester
Use any as a base and connect by train/ bus
Rochester Visitor information
www.visitmedway.org
Youth Hostel Association: Medway (4 miles)
Appendix 4: Tourist Information links

Refreshments
Istead Rise: Co-operative Supermarket
Village Bakers
Cobham: 3 Pubs

Rochester: The Two Brewers
(Shepherd Neame)
Supermarkets, shops, cafes, pubs

Connecting Long Distance Paths
Weald Way
North Downs Way
Medway Valley Walk

Local Paths
The Darnley Trail, Cobham
The City of Rochester Walk
Mill Wood Trail & Cuxton Heritage Trail
Strood Community Trail

Geography
Undulating.
This section is mostly across fields, country
parks and woods and some road walking
through residential and industrial Strood. The
paths through the woods after Cobham can
be muddy and boots are recommended. There
are some wonderful views across the Downs
on this section and a glimpse of the Medway
river towards Maidstone.

Path Profile & Difficulty
Moderate effort.
There are some stiles but footpaths on the
whole are well defined. We maintain height of
around 100 metres into Cobham followed by
gradual climb up to Darnley Mausoleum, the
high point of 135 metres. Down through the
woods to connect with the waymarked North
Downs Way and then an urban and industrial
descent into Strood and Rochester.

Reflections

The reclaimed, regenerated and rejuvenated Jeskyn's Country
Park, yet to reach maturity, can be a bleak beauty - there is little
cover when the wind blows but the Sentinels that guard the
eastern gate will provoke your imagination, the lake attracts
wild life and the paths do the same for the joggers, walkers and
buggy pushers. It feels new but totally unspoilt.

Dickens and Cobham go hand in hand, in fiction and non-
fiction and The Leather Bottle a must for memorabilia but the
Church is worth a visit too as is the 14th century New College.
The Darnley Mausoleum has been restored, but the railings say
'do not touch'. Later, there is the reward of wonderful views over
the valley towards the North Downs. The Strood Community
Trail is the best route available into Rochester giving views of
Rochester, the Castle, Cathedral and the River Medway.

The Walk

Start from the parade of shops, by the bus stop, in the centre of
Istead Rise and head east to the A227. Cross the road into the
lane opposite and follow the track (Footpath Kent CC NU32)
past Ifield Court. This isolated spot has never contained much
more than a manor house, a few buildings and a church but
there has been church here for 700 years, possibly built by

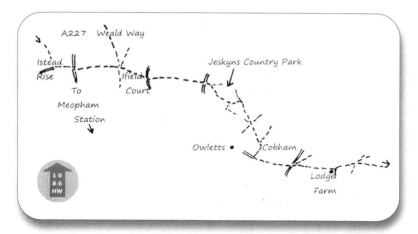

The 'Sentinels' watching over Jeskyns Country Park

pilgrims on their way to Beckett's tomb. The original manor house was moated and the remnants of the moat can still be seen in the dip in front of the house; it would have been full of water when the Master of the house became Lord Mayor of London and Shakespeare walked down the Strand.

The path is on the right just before the Oast houses, cross the field, through the gate and follow the waymarked signs to the road.

Opposite, with electricity pylons marching off into the distance, take the left hand footpath by the hedge that leads to a track between the fields (do not take the path that runs diagonally right across the field).

We are less than ½ a mile south of Watling Street and the high speed rail link into St Pancras. Look back from the top of the hill and the QE II Bridge at Dartford stands proud in the distance.

Cross the road into Jeskyn's Country Park and walk ahead to the gravelled path and turn right. Follow this path as it first curves left through the park and then straightens. Ahead on the horizon, the two 'sentinels' appear, guarding the gateway to Cobham and beyond. They will act as our marker. Bear left again and head for the path that passes between the 'sentinels' and at the gate, look back and they are highlighted against the sky, dominating, demanding and definitely from some future time.

Leave the park and at this point and you have a choice. Either follow the green lane straight ahead and at the kissing gate, turn right and right again, to the well named Battle Street, and on to the junction with The Street and turn left into Cobham. Or if you wish to visit Owletts (NT), turn right and follow the bridle path south (the Darnley Trail) and then left along The Street to Cobham.

Opposite the church is 'The Leather Bottle', with its preserved medieval timber front and famous for its links to Dickens who stayed in Room 6. Dickens calls the Leather Bottle, 'the clean and commodious village ale house' in which stayed the love torn Mr Tracy Tupman of the 'Pickwick Papers' and there is much more Dickens memorabilia inside.

The church is linked closely to the Cobham family, famed for the Cobham brasses, and behind is the New College first endowed by Sir John de Cobham in 1362 and rebuilt in 1598 and I confess that I returned to Cobham later for a wander round the history and a pub lunch.

Next along The Street is 'The Darnley Arms' dating from the Middle Ages, and finally, the Ship Inn, said to have been built from the timbers of a ship wrecked off Sheerness.

At the junction with Halfpence Lane and Cobhambury Road, by the War Memorial, cross into Lodge Lane with the grounds to Cobham Hall on the left.

This road and the following track lead to the Darnley Mausoleum in Cobham Country Park. At the entrance to the Country Park there is a story board and an area for cars to park.

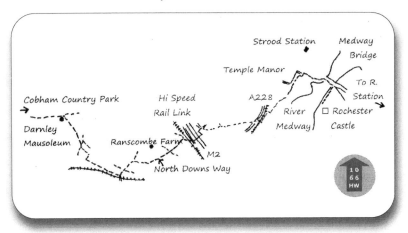

Continue along the track to William's Hill and the Mausoleum. It is unfortunate but there are no spectacular views from this high point and, with nowhere to sit, there is little to keep you here. The Darnley Mausoleum has a commanding position but only commands the trees around it and is locked away behind its fence (is the double padlocked fence there to protect the building from the public or to protect the public from whatever lies 'within'?)

Follow the track round and behind the Mausoleum and at the south east corner there is a waymark sign (look carefully, it can be hidden) for the path downhill through the woods. Keep to this path as it twists and turns, straight on at first junction and at the second, bear right and immediately left. Down into the open, bear right to follow the waymark signs across the field, through the gate at the top, and then bear left and, after a few minutes, unfolding before your eyes is a beautiful view over to the valley below to the wooded Downs in front.

This is idyllic, especially after the disappointment of the Mausoleum, and an ideal stop for lunch sitting on the grass drinking in the view. The footpath is on the left and for those who prefer a little more comfort, just down the path is a clearing and a bench with a similar view albeit not quite so wide ranging.

Continue through the woods, waymarked Ranscombe Farm

The Darnley Mausoleum

Reserve Mill Wood Trail, and at the railway bridge turn left to join the North Downs Way and walk up the snaking path across the Downs in front.

At the drive to Ranscombe Farm, where the NDW turns right, continue straight ahead along the Cuxton Heritage Trail heading for the subway, the M2 and Strood.

When the trees are reached, continue straight ahead, leaving the Cuxton Heritage Trail and take the right hand fork first under the high speed rail link and then the M2 Motorway. Follow the path left and at the top of the rise, turn right and walk in front of the row of houses ahead to Elgin Gardens.

Turn right into Rushdean Road and follow the road downhill for around ten minutes, continuing first into Sycamore Road and then Pilgrims Way, before reaching the A228 Cuxton Road.

Bear left and looking across the A228 is the waymark for the Strood Community Trail that leads to a railway bridge and we

The Saxon Times

Bodiam   12th October 1066

Today with the Saxon Army

From your War Correspondent, embedded with the Saxon Army.

The pace has been relentless.

The Army left the Medway at daybreak. We followed the old Roman road south from Rochester towards Maidstone, up over the ridge crossing the old trackway and down towards the river again and another crossing. There is a settlement there and the bridge is in good condition but it still took some time for the army to cross.

It was a magnificent sight as I watched them go past. It seemed almost two miles from front to back and then there were the wagons and the camp followers.

I saw the King, his brothers and bodyguards ride past. They shouted that they would be at Caldbec tonight to meet the local militia and to set fires alight as if the army was already there. The intention is to mislead William into thinking that we already have the high ground. The rest of the army will arrive tomorrow.

We marched through the Forest of Andreasweald and the old Roman road is in poor condition.

It still cuts through the trees in a straight line and is easy to follow but there are places where the mud is deep between the old banks and occasionally the road stones have been stolen for building.

I've seen a few twisted ankles amongst the men and even broken bones - their war is over, poor sods, and maybe their life if they cannot find a healer quickly.

We push on and on, there is little time to lose as we need to be at the Appledore Estuary by nightfall before the final climb up to 'The Old Hoar Apple Tree' tomorrow.

Everyone I speak to is glad that the King chose the Roman route south.

To move so many men along the old trackways, through Sevenoaks and Tonbridge, would have been difficult at the best of times. Those tracks are unclear, the climbs are steeper, the mud is deeper and only a few are truly confident of knowing their way through the forest.

Tomorrow, we march towards 'The Old Hoar Apple Tree' and my next report will be from Caldbec Hill.

Long Live King Harold II.

The Leather Bottle Cobham, full of Dickens memorabilia

are rewarded with the first views of Rochester Castle. Up and over the bridge and continue straight ahead towards Strood centre, the Medway Bridge and more views of the Castle and the Cathedral.

Follow the path round to the right and at the bottom turn left into the industrial estate and along Knight Road, with Temple Manor (EH) on the right.

The Strood Community Trail passes in front of Morrison's Supermarket, opposite The Alma Inn, and across a wooden bridge turning right, behind the retail park, to continue the waymarked Trail. This final section follows the banks of the river to the Medway Bridge and reveals the very photogenic and dominant Castle, the Cathedral and the Medway in all their splendour. Climb the steps at the end to cross the bridge into Rochester.

The Roman Bridge over the River Medway was roughly on the site of the present bridge and it must have been some feat of engineering 2000 years ago to create a bridge over this tidal river. On the Rochester side would have been the construction camp housing the army, the engineers, the slave labour and all the 'ancillary' services to keep the men happy. No doubt they had targets to meet if only to keep the Generals of their backs. With a plentiful supply of cheap labour, health and safety would not have been an issue, medical care minimal and, no doubt, food carefully rationed as the troops must come first, the slaves can starve.

In time, the camp was reinforced, walls erected, roads, shops and housing built and it became the stronghold 'Durobrivae' and a regional capital. Rochester was born. The Roman Watling Street ran through the centre of the town along what is now Rochester High Street but this walk finishes at Rochester Castle.

After crossing the Medway Bridge turn south for a few yards to the entrance to the Castle, the first Castle to be built by the victorious William after the Battle of Hastings.

Travel Options

a) Rochester Station is a mainline station serving London and East Kent with connections to Strood, Greenhithe, Dartford, Erith, Greenwich and London Terminals. Return to the

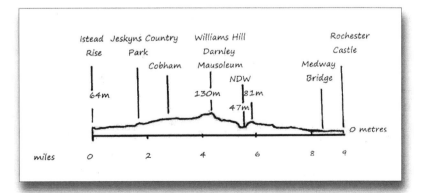

pedestrianised High Street and walk away from the bridge continuing across the junction at the end and follow the signs to the station which is on the left of High Street.

b) Strood Station is back over the Medway Bridge, cross the road into Canal Road and follow the signs to the station. The train from Rochester stops here on the way to London but there are also connections to Maidstone West and Paddock Wood.

Jeskyns Country Park.
Opened in 2007, it was specially created by the Forestry Commission to provide an example of a North Kent natural landscape of orchards, parkland, meadow and woodland. There are trails, wildlife ponds, play areas for the young and amazing sculptures that can dominate a big sky. www.forestry.gov.uk/jeskyns
Jeskyns Country Park Map:
http://www.forestry.gov.uk/pdf/eng-jeskyns-leaflet-map.pdf/$FILE/eng-jeskyns-leaflet-map.pdf

Owletts , NT.
Red brick Charles II house with an interesting garden but restricted opening hours.
http://www.nationaltrust.org.uk/main/w-owletts

Cobham.
Close by is Cobham Park, once a medieval deer park but redesigned by Humphrey Repton, and Cobham Hall, built in the late 16th century on the site of a 12th century manor house. It is now a boarding school but open to visitors on certain days throughout the year. www.cobhamhall.com
There is a Cobham Village Guide available from the church price £2

The Darnley Mausoleum, Cobham Park.
The highest point on this section at 440ft but kept behind bars.
http://www.gravesham.gov.uk/media/pdf/p/r/DarnleyMausoleumLeaflet.pdf
William's Hill relates to the Willman family, late 16th century, rather than Duke William.

Temple Manor EH. www.english-heritage.org.uk/daysout/properties/temple-manor/
Rochester Bridge http://www.rbt.org.uk/bridges/roman.htm
Rochester.
Historic Rochester, for the Romans, an important and strategic centre where Watling Street crossed the River Medway. William built the first castle after the Conquest and it was the scene of Battles in 1215, 1264 and 1667. ('Kent and Sussex Battlefield Walks', Rupert Matthews). The Cathedral is worth visiting for it is both impressive and beautiful. Rochester Castle is now in the hands of English Heritage who publish an excellent guide to the Castle. The town itself has many literary associations with Charles Dickens, links to his novels, Tudor architecture, river walks and enough of interest to want to spend some time exploring - return to do it all justice.

1066 HAROLD'S WAY WALK 6:

ROCHESTER CASTLE TO MAIDSTONE ARCHBISHOP'S PALACE ⟨🚶 Public Footpath⟩

Distance: 12 miles
Time: 5 hours
Maps: OS Explorer: 148

Travel
www.travelinesoutheast.org.uk
Rail
South Eastern services to Strood, Rochester, Maidstone
www.southeasternrailway.co.uk
Parking
Strood: Pay and Display
Rochester: Pay and Display
Maidstone: Pay and Display

Connecting Long Distance Paths
North Downs Way
Medway Valley Walk
Saxon Shore Way
Pilgrims Way
Riverside Walk, Maidstone
(for Weblinks, see Appendix 4)

Accommodation
London, Rochester, Maidstone
Use any as a base and connect by train
Youth Hostel Association: Medway (4 miles)
Appendix 4: Tourist Information links

Allington Lock: Premier Inn (next to The Malta Inn)

Maidstone: Innkeeper's Lodge
(next to The White Rabbit)
Caravan Club. Bearstead, Maidstone– 4 miles

Refreshments
Blue Bell Hill:
Robin Hood
Cobtree Manor Park:
Cobtree Cabin (open daily to 3pm, toilets)
Allington Lock:
The Malta Inn
Maidstone:
Wide variety including:
The White Rabbit
Drakes Cork and Cask

Geography.
A combination of river walks and the North Downs Way with far reaching views over the Medway valley.

Path Profile & Difficulty
Moderate.
After Rochester, there is a steady climb along the North Downs Way up to the Robin Hood PH (165 metres), a short descent and then a climb to Blue Bell Hill Picnic Area (185 metres), with a final walk down into the Medway Valley to Maidstone. There are some stiles and the ground may be muddy in wet weather.

Reflections

On the day that I walked up onto the North Downs from Rochester, small planes seemed to be enjoying the freedom of the skies. The sound of their engines howling as they dived and climbed created an illusion of war. The somnolent Medway valley below this strategic ridge appears peaceful but long before the Battle of Britain it shaped the future of England. The Medway River drew a line against invading foes at the Battles of Medway and Aylesford. Later, the Battles of Rochester and Maidstone defined political struggles caused by civil wars.

Significantly, Aylesford (AD455) allowed the Saxons to secure their foothold in Kent. It was the beginning of a dynasty that would last for some 600 years and end with the defeat of Harold.

At Allington Lock, there are old Thames barges, Dutch barges and sailing barges amidst the cabin cruisers. The 'Allington Belle' glides by the willows takings its cargo of passengers from the Malta Inn to Maidstone, suitably refreshed - £5 return.

The Walk

Standing at the entrance to Rochester Castle, face the Medway and turn left to walk by the side of the River, following the waymark signs for the Medway Valley Walk and the Saxon Shore Way. We are leaving Watling Street and opting for the quiet of the North Downs Way and the river bank rather than the Roman road that Harold took to Blue Bell Hill –now the busy A229.

Continue by the side of the river as it curves past the development of riverside flats and you approach an area that was once the Short Brothers Seaplane Factory. The ramp into the Medway can still be seen and allowed them to launch the seaplanes straight into the river. The planes built here are synonymous with both World Wars but the factory closed in 1948. In the late 1990's, the site was cleared for re-development.

At Shorts Way, take the footpath on the right into Batty's Marsh, Borstal Local Reserve. Although half a mile from the motorway with its bridge rising high above the River, the roar

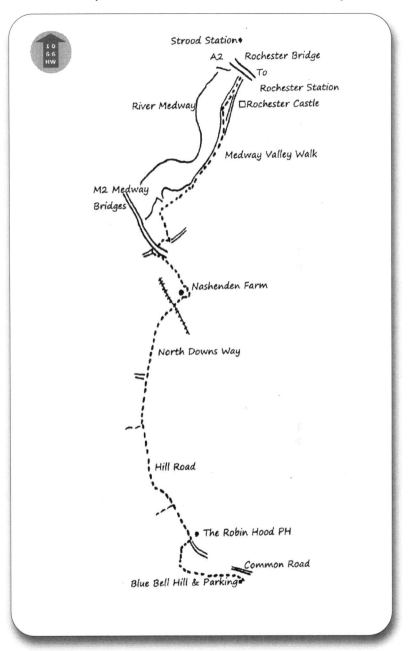

of the traffic can be heard. I have already had enough of traffic but it will be three miles before the traffic noise gives way to the birdsong of the North Downs Way.

Continue along the waymarked Medway Valley Walk, take the path to the left of the gates at Medway Bridge Marina and after a couple of minutes, look for the path on the left up the hill. At the top, turn right along Wouldham Road, under the motorway, then left into Nashenden Farm Lane waymarked the North Downs Way.

Down from the Robin Hood PH

We will stay on the North Downs Way for around five miles before the final descent to the River Medway and a peaceful walk along the riverbank to Maidstone.

Turn right at Nashenden Farm, crossing the bridge over the Eurostar rail link and through the gates, following the waymarks, to start the short climb up onto the Downs. Here there are good views over the Medway Valley and to the North Downs that continue westwards. We looked over to this point as we approached Ranscombe Farm in Walk 5 and finally, it is quiet again except for the wind in the trees.

Continue past the Shoulder of Mutton Wood which hides a round barrow and confirms that people were living on the Downs from at least the Bronze Age and perhaps before. We are not the first to walk here but walking poles have replaced spears, technical gear the skins and furs and lunch is wrapped in clingfilm instead of running wild. Imagination makes up for the fact that we are a little distance from the Roman road and the route that Harold would have taken.

The climb continues through the trees with little or no view until, on the right, there is a clearing, a picnic table and a bench and after 1¼ hours it is an ideal place for a break.

Down below, looking south at the bend in the river, King Caratacus and his army faced the Roman invasion at the Battle of Medway in AD43. The battle site is presumed to be by the River at Burham and it is possible that the army of Caratacus numbered well over 100,000. All the same, he was defeated by the smaller but more disciplined Roman army and the first phase of the Roman conquest of Britain was complete.

Walking on and on the left is a rare break in the trees with a view north west towards the Thames estuary. I had imagined that I would be walking along an open ridge and lord of all I survey but this is not the case and the area is still heavily wooded, as it has been for centuries.

After almost five miles, we reach the lane on the left leading to the hidden Robin Hood PH. Turn right, the sign says 'Byway Path 21', and down the hill, and although we are losing height it is a more rewarding route than the slog of hot tarmac to the Blue Bell Hill Picnic Area.

As the gradient reduces and the path bears to the right, there is an opening in the trees with a bench and a view over the valley towards the western North Downs. The path to Blue Bell Hill and Burham Downs is just behind you. It was here that I met the West Maidstone 'Very Active' Retirement Group, Kent CC, out on a ramble. They became a captive audience for a quick history of 1066 Harold's Way. You can never miss an opportunity for a bit of self-promotion but they did suggest that I took the track through Burham Downs rather than continue on the footpath. Good advice, there are better views over the trees as you walk through the chalk grass land, but the track is narrow.

Perhaps Plautius and his Roman legions camped here overlooking the meandering Medway River before the battle. It was not an easy victory for the Romans as Caratacus lived to fight another day.

Rejoin the main path and continue the steady climb up the hill through the trees to bear left at the junction with the path from Burham village. At the next junction, continue straight ahead through the overhanging branches of the wood. The path is sunken here, reasonably wide and could be evidence of an older road or track worn down by traffic from the top of the hill to Burham. We will see many similar paths along 1066 Harold's Way.

Towards the top of the hill, bear right at the waymark sign to the Blue Bell Hill Picnic Area. As the path opens out, there are benches with views or you can walk the few more metres to the picnic tables and to my ideal lunch stop at this the halfway point. There are no better views over the Medway. Look south towards Maidstone and you can trace the route after lunch. Blue Bell Hill really is a commanding spot, close to the old Roman road and 1066 Harold's Way south.

South west is Aylesford and the site of the Battle of Aylesford, AD455.

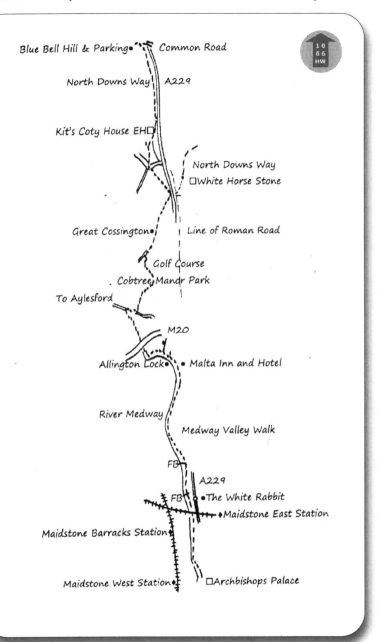

Blue Bell Hill & Parking• Common Road

North Downs Way | A229

Kit's Coty House EH□

North Downs Way
□White Horse Stone

Great Cossington• | Line of Roman Road

Golf Course
. Cobtree Manor Park

To Aylesford

M20
Allington Lock• • Malta Inn and Hotel

River Medway

Medway Valley Walk

FB
A229
FB •The White Rabbit
•Maidstone East Station

Maidstone Barracks Station•

Maidstone West Station• □Archbishops Palace

At Kit's Coty House

In the aftermath of the Roman recall, Britain came under increasing attacks from the Picts and Celts that threatened the new independent government. An 'invitation' was issued to Hengist, a feared and famous Saxon mercenary, to come and sort out this little local problem and a place was found for the Saxon Army to live – Kent! Peace reigned but the government grew weary of paying for protection and after the gold and silver stipend was stopped, trouble brewed.

The Saxons turned to a bit of murder, looting and pillage to collect their dues, destroying towns and cities, creating mayhem and instability, and returning to Kent to promptly declare independence. The resulting battle, although fought to a draw, allowed the Saxons to stay in England. It was a defining moment in English history heralding the start of the 600 year Anglo-Saxon dynasty that ended with Harold's defeat in 1066.

The North Downs Way continues from the bottom east point

of the car park, just over the lip. Follow the North Downs Way downhill, parallel with the main road, and bear right onto the slip road for the A229. After approximately 400 metres, turn right to follow a footpath finger post down steps, losing height quickly. It makes us aware of just how far we had climbed up from Rochester.

Keep your eyes open on the right for a gap in the hedge through which you can see Kit's Coty House (EH), three uprights and a massive capstone that are all that is left of former megalithic burial chamber.

At the end of the path, cross the road into the Pilgrims Way and North Downs Way, to meet up once again with the A229. Turn right, towards the electricity pylon.

Horsa, the brother of Hengest, died at the Battle of Aylesford, and the White Horse Stone is said to mark his burial site. To visit, follow the NDW for about a third of a mile under the A229, over the Railway Bridge and the stone is a little way up the path into the trees. To return to 1066 Harold's Way just reverse your steps.

Back on 1066 Harold's Way and head towards the pylon where the footpath and stile are on the right. Into the field, keeping the hedge on your right, and as the hedge bends to the left, look right for the waymark and follow the path through the trees, into the next field. At the road turn right through the little collection of houses and farms that make up Great Cossington.

As the lane bends right, take the waymarked path left towards the golf course. Although the path is straight ahead across the course, I chose to avoid the errant golf balls driven by wayward golfers and turned right at this point along the wide, clear and well maintained path/ track that runs on the outside of the golf course through the trees.

Keep following the path round to the left with its occasional glimpses of Blue Bell Hill and at the path junction, turn right away from the course and up a slight rise into Cobtree Manor Park.

At the top, bear right along the broad bridleway, keeping the wire fence to the right.

After around 220 metres, as the 'Bridleway' turns left, continue straight ahead, down the slope left, through the trees for 40 metres, to turn right along the 'Woodland Walk'. Continue along Woodland Walk as it first bends to the right and then turns left down a track bordered by logs to the Picnic Area, Cobtree Cabin, Car Park and toilets.

Leave the Park through the main gates and turn right, crossing the busy road and in between the Builders Merchants and the Car Showroom is the sign for the Public Footpath down to the Medway. At the end, turn left and join the Medway Valley Walk to Allington Lock, passing under the M20.

There is a marina on the opposite bank and boats in and out of the water and, despite the road noise in the background, it feels a tranquil place enveloped by the timelessness and stillness of the river, the ducks floating by, the overhanging willows, meadows and dappled sunlight.

Others thought so too for there is history of settlement. The ancient Britons, built a moated village, the Romans a villa, the Saxons a moated stronghold, the Normans a manor house and finally in the 13thcentury, the manor house was fortified into Allington Castle.

The Roman road, south from Rochester, touches the river at this point and you can believe that Harold would have been welcomed and more than likely joined by additional soldiers for the battle ahead.

The story board on the approach to the car park describes the Medway Valley Walk and has information about the Lock, the first of which was built in 1792 at this the tidal limit of the Medway. The Malta Inn is in a superb spot next to the river at Allington Lock and with just over two miles left to Maidstone it maybe worth a stop on a sunny day - if you can find a table outside. There are boats and barges moored and it is a staging point for pleasure cruises from Maidstone. The river does have a beauty here and the opportunity for a rest at the Malta Inn is too good to miss. *If the Allington Belle is running it is possible to buy a single to The Archbishop's Palace in Maidstone, the finish of this section. Complete the walk in style with a riverboat cruise, if your conscience allows.*

Allington Castle is across the river, once the home of Sir Thomas Wyatt who was executed in 1554, at the Tower of London, for his part in the rebellion against Queen Mary at the Battles of Wrotham and of Cooling.

Follow the river path into Maidstone to the Archbishop's Palace. It is a peaceful and fitting end to our walk and unless you have a train to catch there is no need to rush.

Under the two road bridges and in the shadow of the Archbishop's Palace, All Saints Church and the College there is a chance to rest our feet on a bench next to the river. There are story boards, here and in the grounds, that recount the history of the area which stretches back to the 13thcentury. We have

Looking along the Medway towards the Archbishop's Palace - the finish is just by the riverboat

passed the quay for the 'Allington Belle' and are close to Mill Street and High Street, the scene of fierce fighting between the Royalists and the Parliamentarians in 1648.

The old Roman road, now the pedestrianised Week Street and Gabriel's Hill, led Harold to the crossing of the River Len. Harold continued his march south, first along the line of the old A229 and then in the direction of Chart Sutton. Lower and Upper Stone Streets are further reminders of the Roman road. We catch up with Harold again on the Roman Brishing Lane

The next section, Maidstone to Staplehurst, starts here continuing along the riverbank before entering the Loose Valley. Roman roads beckon and we will be following in the footsteps of Harold, down from the ragstone ridge and across the Low Weald.

For The White Rabbit: after the second footbridge on the approach to Maidstone, continue along the river path for around 50 metres. Ignore the first path sharp left but take the second path, by the Maidstone Invicta Rowing Club that leads into James Wathan Way. Continue to the traffic island and across the busy A229 stands The White Rabbit, less than a ¼ mile from Maidstone East Station.

Maidstone East: Alternatively, at the railway bridge, there are steps and a bridge across the busy A229. Take the footpath into Brenchley Gardens, with its links to the Battle of Maidstone and to Maidstone East Railway Station for the train to London Victoria.

Drakes Cork and Cask: On the approach to the first road bridge, there is an underpass, left, that leads to Drakes Cork and Cask.

Travel

There are of three Stations in Maidstone, Maidstone East, next to Brenchley Gardens, has connections to London Terminals and East Kent whereas Maidstone Barracks and Maidstone West link Rochester and Paddock Wood.

For Hastings and East Sussex, Maidstone is the terminus for Arriva Service 5 to Hawkhurst and links to Hastings and Battle.

The Bus Stop is on King Street. From the Archbishop's Palace walk through the gardens to the A229 and cross the road at this busy junction into Mill Street. At the top of Mill Street, turn right into High Street and continue until it becomes King Street.

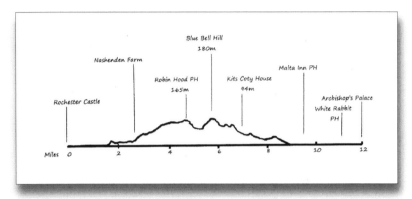

The excellent **'Battlefield Walks Kent and Sussex'** by **Rupert Matthews** covers the following battles in detail and is well worth the read
- Battles of Rochester, 1215, 1264, 1667
- Battle of Medway, AD43 - Blue Bell Hill
- Battle of Aylesford, 455 - Kit's Coty House (EH), White Horse Stone, Hengest and Horsa.
- Battles of Wrotham and of Cooling, both 1554

Shorts Factory, Rochester.
We walk past the old landing stage of this famous factory that made aircraft for both World Wars that included the Sunderland Flying Boat. There are exhibits relating to the factory in Rochester's Guildhall Museum (High Street) and old photographs of the planes are posted at: www.kenthistoryforum.co.uk/index.php?topic=3646.30 and http://www.medwaylines.com/shortbrothers.htm

Borstal
An irony in the name that means a place of security and refuge, similar to Bostall Woods of Walk 2, but Borstal entered the English language again for a different reason. The reform of the prison system in the late 19th century led to the creation of an institute for boys who got into trouble, separating them from the prison system. The first institution opening at Borstal in 1902 and the name became generic, lasting for 80 years.
Away from the path is St Matthews, built in 1878, famous for its seven sanctuary lamps
www.stmatthewsborstal.co.uk/church/index.php?option=com_content&view=article&id=46&Itemid=28

Cobtree Manor Park

For a map of Cobtree Manor Park visit: http://cobtreepark.co.uk/

Allington

This is the point where the Medway ceases to be tidal and the locks here are a vital part of the flood control scheme for the Medway valley. The lock also ensures that there is sufficient water for the Medway to remain navigable up to Maidstone and beyond.

Allington Belle http://www.allingtonbelle.co.uk/

Maidstone

Maidstone was on the route of the Roman road from Rochester to Hastings, (Margary route 13) and a crossing point over the River Medway and River Len.

There is evidence of Roman and Anglo-Saxon settlement and Maidstone later developed from a market town into the county town of Kent and until the early 20th century it was a flourishing inland port.

The town was laid out in the late 11th and 12th centuries with the Archbishop's Palace, All Saints Church and the College dating from the 14th century and they are better seen from the river banks than from the road. Brenchley Gardens is at the entrance to Maidstone East Station and contains the rebuilt St Faith's Church. In 1648, the Church was the Royalist command centre at the Battle of Maidstone and it saw the surrender of the Royalist army. http://www.tour-maidstone.com/

Battle of Maidstone, 1st June, 1648

Not everybody was happy with the Parliamentary reforms –the suppression of traditional Christmas celebrations was not a vote winner –

and there was a call for the King to be re-instated. Rioting took place in several places in the country, and a Royalist rebellion broke out in Kent centred on Maidstone. Although the Royalists numbered around 15,000, they were poorly trained and up against the Parliamentary Army, led by Sir Thomas Fairfax, who advanced on Maidstone from the direction of East Farleigh and Tovil. The Battle was fought around Mill Street, what is now the A229, and then into the town itself with the Royalist army retreating to St Faith's Church and surrendering later that night. The Battle of Maidstone marked the final end of the Civil War.

1066 HAROLD'S WAY WALK 7:
MAIDSTONE TO STAPLEHURST

Distance: 10.50 miles
(detour at Lambs Cross adds ¼ mile)
Time: 4 hours
Maps: OS Explorer:148 & 136

Travel
www.travelinesoutheast.org.uk
Rail
South Eastern:
London, Maidstone, Staplehurst
www.southeasternrailway.co.uk
Bus
Arriva Service 5:
Maidstone, Staplehurst, Sandhurst

Parking
Maidstone: Car Parks
Staplehurst: Station Car Park
Pay and Display

Accommodation
Maidstone: see Walk 6
Staplehurst: Weald Cottage B and B
Appendix 4: Tourist Information links

Refreshments
Maidstone: Wide variety
Loose: The Chequers PH
Rabbit's Cross: Lord Raglan PH
Staplehurst: Railway Tavern
Staplehurst Café
Old Staplehurst: King's Head
Bell Inn

Connecting Long Distance Paths
Medway Valley Walk
Greensand Way

Geography
From the start by the River Medway, the path leads into the splendid Loose Valley Conservation Area. There is the climb up to Quarry Hills and a walk along the ragstone ridge between the North Downs and the Weald (up to 110 metres). The descent into the Weald is along the route of the old Roman road into mainly arable and grazing land.

Path Profile & Difficulty
Moderate.
There is a short steady climb on the approach to the Loose Valley and again leaving Loose. The next section is flat to gently undulating with some stiles and gates followed by the descent from the ridge along the route of the Roman road and into Chart Hill Road. The final section is flat across fields into Staplehurst. Many of the paths and bridleways appear to have been used for centuries. Footpaths are reasonably clear but are not always waymarked and you will need to take care as repairs are required to some of the bridges and stiles. Across the Weald, there is some road walking involved but it is along the line of the old Roman road.

Reflections

It must have been blessed relief for the horses pulling heavy Roman wagons, filled with lead or stone, and for the soldiers of Rome and of King Harold to finally arrive at the Low Weald. A few miles of flat land would ease the aching legs of the army after the climb up and over the North Downs.

The outline of the Roman road remains visible on its descent from the ragstone ridge, from the Quarry Hills into the Low Weald. Imagination echoes to the footsteps of countless legionnaires, the rattle of wagons and the shouts of the Saxon army.

But first, a quiet stroll along the River Medway to leave Maidstone before entering the jewel that is the Loose Valley Conservation Area. There can be no more beautiful start to a walk, along the valley lanes and paths of the River Loose, a river that still has the power to drive the mill wheels of the old paper mills. The photogenic entry into Loose provides a fitting end to the first three miles and there is a danger that you may not stray further than The Chequers.

The Walk

Start by the River Medway, at the gateway to the Archbishop's Palace. Walk along the river by the side of the Palace to the footbridge at the bottom of Horseway. Cross the river and walk westwards away from the town along the metalled path.

Looking back from the bridge for the best view of the 14th century Church and Archbishop's Palace and, in front, to the large sculpture of a stag by Edward Bainbridge Copnall, moved from Stag Place, London in 2004.

This is the Lockmeadow Path, part of the River Medway Valley Path that continues to Tonbridge and joins with the Wealdway and the Eden Valley Walk. The riverside is being developed with flats built on both sides as Maidstone extends its boundaries – the canoeists, reflected in the mirror like river, will have to paddle a little further before they find open countryside, although the blackberries growing by the river are free from pollution and at

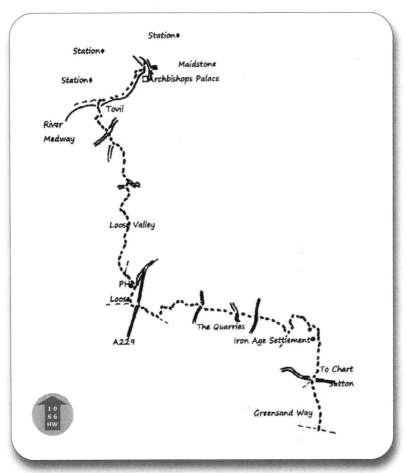

the end of August should be ripe for picking.

The anglers seem to be here for peace rather than sport – all very professional but I haven't seen anything caught, still time I suppose, it's only midday.

After half a mile cross the blue footbridge, walk up Wharf Road and turn right at the junction into Lower Tovil. Cross the road and take second left, Bridgeside Mews, and bear left to follow the Public Footpath by the side of the houses.

This short gloomy section, between the houses and the back

of factories, provides a sharp contrast to the splendour of the Loose Valley, less than half a mile away.

At Tovil Hill, cross the road and walk up Straw Mill Hill turning left into the narrow, pathless Cave Hill – take care. Trees provide a cathedral arch to walk through and ivy overhangs the wall, iron railings mark the boundary of the road as we descend towards the River Loose. At one time, there were 13 mills along the valley and the river is a series of mill ponds cascading down like rapids.

Continue along this road for ½ a mile with the river on the left. There are story boards describing the Loose Valley Conservation area and some of the history of the river and its mills. We are so close to Maidstone and yet so far away in time and it gets better. There is a working water wheel at Upper

Looking back at the Archbishop's Palace

Crisbrook Mill and Hayle Mill is reflected in the enormous mill pond.

At Hayle Mill Cottages, where the road meets Teasaucer Hill, turn right along Bockingford Lane, signposted Coxheath and East Farleigh, of Maidstone Battle fame. Over the river and turn left, signposted Great Ivy, to continue along the Loose River. At the story board that identifies 'The Loose Valley Conservation Area', bear left to follow the waymarked signs.

We are some way away from the route that Harold took but the A229 is too busy to be enjoyable and this section, through the beautiful Loose Valley, is too idyllic to be missed – it really is a gem and full credit to the Loose Valley Conservation team for all their work. Even after a heavy rain storm, this section is still firm underfoot.

Continue by the side of the river through a swing gate and into a dark path beneath overhanging trees to enter Loose along Kirkdale. At the junction with Bridge Street and Church Street turn left. This path, by the very picturesque and photogenic stream, thoroughly deserves a photograph and the scene is completed by 'The Chequers' in front but it is too early to stop and there is another 8 miles to go – pity, for the food and beer are good.

Turn right and with the Chequers on your right walk up the hill in front signposted Coxheath (take care, again no paths). This used to be the main A229 before the village, and the hills both sides of the Chequers, were bypassed. Towards the top of Old Loose Hill, turn left, towards the busy A229 and the path opposite.

We have now completed most of the climb out of Maidstone and the route now roughly follows the ridge to meet up with the old Roman road near Chart Sutton and then down into the Low Weald.

After 50 metres, climb the stile on the right and follow the waymarked path across the field and continue ahead into Salts Lane. As Salts Lane turns right, take the bridleway left down the hill and ignore the tempting broad public footpath ahead.

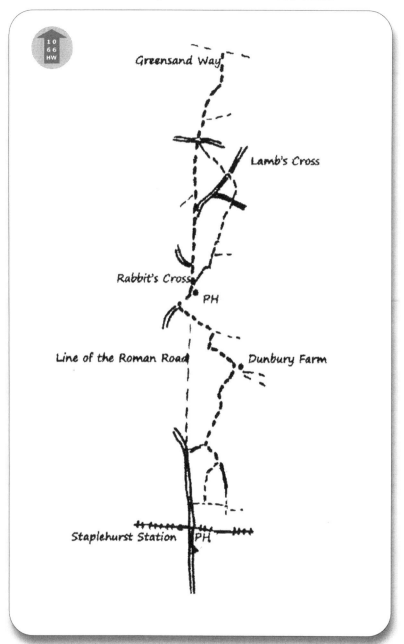

The unspoilt Horseway, Maidstone

The bridleway becomes a path between overgrown hedges and leads, twisting and turning, to a track that appears to have once been paved with stone. On reaching the wooden post on the right, identifying the limit of the 'Loose Valley Conservation Area', take the path straight ahead as the track bears left.

At Bottlescrew Hill turn right up the hill, left at the junction and right into 'The Quarries'. This area again has a village atmosphere and although we are using roads, it is peaceful. The Romans quarried stone 2000 years ago and there is some interesting history of the area on the Boughton Monchelsea website.

Cross the road at the end and continue east, along the public bridleway, over the next road and follow the path, by the side of a stream, rising through the trees. The path levels out and at the end of the fence, it is important to bear left and follow the path through the fields to Brishing Road. Do not continue

straight ahead, it just leads deeper and deeper into the dark
wood and goes nowhere. I know.

At Brishing Road turn right and we are now back on the route
of the old Roman road. At the junction with the B2163 cross
over to continue along Brishing Road and at the end, look left
and take the bridleway opposite.

A scene from the Bayeux Tapestry shows Duke William of Normandy
(left) giving arms to Earl Harold Godwinsson during Harold's visit to
Normandy in 1064. The two men would meet in battle in 1066.

Descending south from the ridge, the evidence of the Roman road becomes more apparent. There are similar green lanes between Sissinghurst and Bodiam that follow the same Roman road.

The Greensand Way crosses 1066 Harold's Way and after 6½ miles, and perhaps 2¼ hours, it is time to stop. Up the stone steps to the right and the land opens out into an orchard and a meadow, an ideal spot and perhaps the only spot to rest and have lunch looking out over the Low Weald south towards Staplehurst.

Rejoin the path and in summer, if you are lucky, there are blackberries worth picking well away from pollution, a mouth watering feast that hits the spot on a hot day. Head down the hill and at the crossroads there are options:

1. Continue along the road in front for 1½ miles. This is the Roman road that Harold travelled along and an opportunity to stride out at marching pace with perhaps the theme from 'Gladiator' playing on your MP3. We have only 3½ miles left on this section but for Harold and his army there were still 25 miles to march and then to prepare for battle.

Look out for the Wealden Hall house, all angles and odd shapes but it has surprisingly stood for centuries - it is associated with a Thomas Rabbet, 1613, rather than the fluffy bunnies that I had in mind.

2. If you wish to avoid the road, the alternative route is across the fields but it does miss out on the Roman march.

At the crossroads at the bottom of the hill, look to the left of the road ahead and there is a footpath sign obscured by the electricity pole. Through the gate and walk across the field in the direction of the waymark, aim to the right of the middle tree and follow the path through the crops to the stile, over the fence ahead, and in to the next field. Follow the waymarks to the gate in the top right corner of the field and into the lane by the entrance to Lamb's Cross Farm. It would appear that this is a satisfactory diversion to the path shown on the OS Explorer 136.

Cross the road into Green Lane and at the crossroads, the footpath continues over the stile to the right of the entrance to Chart Hall Farm. Follow the waymarks, firstly keeping the hedge to your left and as the hedge turns left, continue straight ahead across the field to a gate and more waymarks. Keep the hedge to your right and in June, the hedgerow is alive with briar roses in flower, perfect. Over the stile, head straight across the field, across a paddock following the path to the top right corner and exit into a lane, turn right to rejoin the main road and turn left to pick up the route for Option 1.

Walk towards and 'past' the isolated 'Lord Raglan' pub. It is featured in the Daily Telegraph Kent Pub Guide and it is as good as the review but once you enter the doors you may find it difficult to leave.

Two hundred metres after the Lord Raglan take the lane on the left, between the entrances to Ringinglow and Chaney Court Farm, the footpath sign is hidden in the hedge by the electricity pole. Walk for around 15 minutes to Dunbury Oast where the waymark for the path is by the gate next to the entrance to the Oast. Through the gate, over the bridge and follow the track, straight ahead, over another rough bridge to continue to the stile in the top left hand corner of the field.

Follow the waymark signs by the side of the field and after about 100 metres look for the next waymark tacked to a tree in the hedge on the left. If you miss it, it is a big field to walk around! Turn right towards the two oak trees* in the middle and on through the gap in the hedge ahead. Continue in the same direction, SSW, first by the hedge and then across the next field heading for the gate to the left of the house ahead and into Couchman Green Lane. *(*These two trees are all that remain of the field boundary that is shown on the OS Explorer 136).*

Here the peace and quiet that we have enjoyed is now broken by the sound of the traffic from the A229 and the occasional warning signal from trains on the mainline approaching the Staplehurst station.

Turn left and walk along the lane and as the lane bears round to the right, take the footpath right, over the bridge and the stile and continue across the field keeping the hedge to the left and then in between the hedge and the fence to the stile in the top left hand corner.

Follow the waymarks, keeping the hedge to the right, and continue until the path connects with the path from Couchman Greens Lane to the A229. Turn right, over the stile and continue through paddocks to the A229.

Look right and the sign for Weald Cottage B&B can be seen just past the 40mph sign

Turn left and the A229 leads to the welcoming Railway Tavern. The finish at Station Approach is convenient for the bus to Maidstone, Hawkhurst and Hastings, train connections to London Bridge and East Kent and car parking. The Roman road continues through the centre of Staplehurst towards Cranbrook.

Loose village looking towards The Chequers

Rabbits Cross - all angles and odd shapes

Loose
Of Saxon origin, the village later harnessed the power of the fast flowing River Loose
to support a paper making industry that peaked during the Industrial Revolution. The
little river now provides a focal point for this unique village. For further information
and history, http://www.infobritain.co.uk/Loose_And_Loose_Valley.htm
Boughton Monchelsea
Although the village is not on our route, the parish covers the Kent ragstone quarries
dominating the ridge above Maidstone that date back to the Roman era. An earlier Iron
Age settlement lies close to the route of the old Roman road. http://www.boughton-
monchelsea-pc.org.uk/index.php?option=com_content&view=article&id=53&Itemid
=60

Greensand Way

This was a major east-west route following the sandstone ridge lying to the north of the chalk downs. Although an old trackway, the Romans used it to link the south-east ports with Stane Street. It also crossed both the Hassocks to London and the Lewes, Brighton to London Roman roads. Greensand Way is 108 miles long and stretches from Haslemere in Surrey through to Hamstreet in Kent. Details can be found at:www.kent.gov.uk
leisure_and_culture/countryside_and_coast/walking/greensand_way

Staplehurst

Staplehurst, meaning Post Wood, lies on the route of the old Roman road, now part of the A229 and at one time referred to as 'The Great Road'.

In June 1865, the train from Folkestone to London approached the viaduct over the River Beult close to Staplehurst. The red warning flag was shown too late and the train, travelling at about 50 mph, was derailed over the viaduct with 10 dead and 49 injured. Charles Dickens was a passenger in the seventh carriage and came close to losing his life and it is said that he never fully recovered from his ordeal.

At the Cranbrook end of the village, on a slight hill, is an older Staplehurst with cottages gathered round the church next to the Bell Inn and the Kings Arms. Some are said to date from the 15th and 16th centuries and one is rumoured to have Saxon detail. Do not be fooled by the Crown House, it is too good to be true!
 http://www.staplehurstvillage.org.uk/visitor_information.aspx
http://www.britishlistedbuildings.co.uk/england/kent/staplehurst

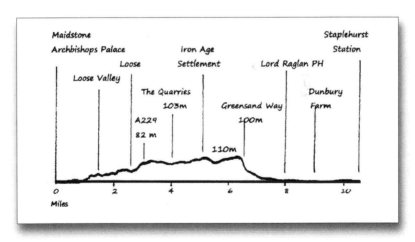

1066 HAROLD'S WAY WALK 8:

STAPLEHURST TO SISSINGHURST VIA SISSINGHURST CASTLE ⚇ Public Footpath ⟩

Distance: 10.65 miles
Time: 4 hours
Maps: OS Explorer: 136 & 137

Travel
www.travelinesoutheast.org.uk
Rail
South Eastern to Staplehurst
www.southeasternrailway.co.uk
Bus
Arriva Service 5:
Maidstone to Sandhurst via Staplehurst and
Sissinghurst village*
Parking
Staplehurst: On street
Station Car Park: Pay & Display
Sissinghurst Castle: NT Car Park
Sissinghurst: On Street

*Sissinghurst Castle to Bus Stop: 1¼ miles
Allow 30 minutes*

Accommodation
Staplehurst, Sissinghurst Castle, Cranbrook
Maidstone, Hastings and St Leonards,
Appendix 4: Tourist Information links

Refreshments
Staplehurst: Various shops and pubs
Knoxbridge: Knoxbridge Café
Open Mon to Sat 7.30am - 2 pm
Hop Bine Inn – restricted hours

Sissinghurst Castle:
National Trust tearooms
Sissinghurst: Convenience store

Connecting Long Distance Paths
None

Geography
This is a typical Kentish Wealden walk amidst
meadow, fields, meandering streams, woods
and the remnants of water mills. A journey
across the undulating Low Weald from
Staplehurst before climbing up to Hocker Edge
(370ft) and a final walk on tracks and lanes
to Sissinghurst Castle.

Path Profile & Difficulty
Undulating. Moderate.
There are stiles and the occasional kissing
gate. Footpaths are not always well defined
and the waymarks can be hard to spot on this
walk. The first part is mostly through
meadow which makes for a very pleasant
walk although paths can be muddy. There is a
steady climb up to Hocker Edge and only a
little road walking along the country lanes
where traffic is minimal.
There is the opportunity to spend time visiting
Sissinghurst Castle (National Trust). The
Castle is just over a mile from the centre of
the village and 1¼ miles from the bus stop in
Sissinghurst village.

Reflections

"Quick, quicker, we need to make good time, 4½ miles to Sissinghurst and 12 miles to Bodiam. You can see the road is straight, straight through the forest. Pick up your feet, you can rest at the estuary, the camp for tonight."

But we can dawdle through the fields and meadows that make up the Low Weald and look back from Hocker Edge across the valley to a rural England at its best. Old Staplehurst sits on a hill, clustered around the church next to the A229, the old Roman road. It was a Saxon settlement and part of Kent House, next to the Bell, is said to date from Saxon times.

Stroll through peaceful meadows by the stream, but turn into the valley at Hartridge and the stream changes character into a medieval industrial powerhouse for long gone corn mills, fed by rushing water from header lakes further up the valley. One steepish climb to Hocker Ridge and although Sissinghurst Castle is away from the Roman road, it would be irresponsible to miss these famous gardens before the finish at Sissinghurst and it's bus stops to Maidstone and Hastings.

The Walk

This section starts at Station Approach, Staplehurst, on the A229 Hawkhurst to Maidstone Road, outside the Railway Tavern, and is convenient for both the station and Arriva bus service 5.

The road south continues on to the centre and the older part of Staplehurst along the line of the Roman road south and Harold's route but it is a mile long slog through a built up area.

Leaving the Railway Tavern, walk south along the A229 for a few metres and take the first road left, Fishers Road and continue to the end and into the footpath, left, by the fence. Keep the fence to your right and at the end, turn right behind the oast house and the garage unit, and follow the waymarked path through the trees and between the ponds into the paddock beyond.

Follow the field round left to the gate opposite and continue

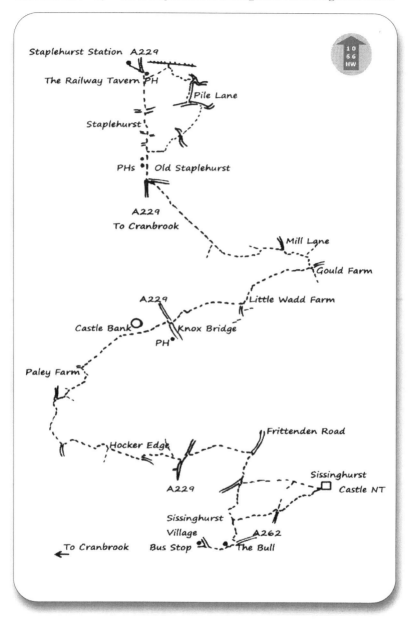

into the next field and again follow the second field round left to and through a kissing gate. Opposite, across the field, is the exit into Couchman Greens Lane. Just be aware that each time I have walked this starting section there have been horses and ponies in these three fields and fences electrified but with safe crossing points.

Turn immediately right into Pile Lane, past the greyhound track on the left and at the main road turn left and walk towards the Jubilee Sports Field. Opposite the entrance is the footpath that stretches away to the right, towards Old Staplehurst, and on the horizon are the chimneys to Spilsill Court, originally built in the 13th C.

At Spilsill Farm, continue straight ahead across the bridge, over the track and along the clear path, with views of Staplehurst Church to the left. On into Chapel Lane and at the A229 turn left towards All Saints Church.

Over the brow of the hill, we pass both the Kings Head and the Bell Inn but it is too early to stop. Kent House is next to The Bell.

Look for Frittenden Road on the left and the footpath runs diagonally south east from the junction, by the side of the playing fields.

Where the iron gate bars the path, look right for the footpath waymark stone to follow the path by the side of Staplehurst Manor.

Over the stile (do not take the left hand fork) and continue straight across the field to the gate opposite and follow the waymark signs heading for the top left corner of the field - along the faint track in the grass. At the next stile, turn right through the field opening and bear left - the waymark directs you diagonally across the field to a gate that leads to a path between the trees.

Continue the path straight ahead keeping Maplehurst Wood to the left. Frittenden Church appears on the horizon and down in the valley, to the right, is Gould Farm Oast House which will soon be passed.

Exit the field through the gate into Mill Lane and turn right and follow the lane until a sharp left hand bend and turn right into the drive next to Gould Farm. Follow the track and green lane past the oast house and on leaving the next field take the right hand fork. The waymark is just around the bend to the left and directs the path across the field, through the crops heading for the large grain storage units ahead. This is Fridays (Cranbrook) Ltd land whom we can thank for such a clear path.

Bear left at the end, to meander through the trees towards Little Wadd Farm. The path becomes a drive and when the drive meets the metalled lane, turn right along the clearly marked path between the trees, heading due west.

At the end of the path, turn left along the drive, away from the Fridays Grain Store to reach the busy A229, at the Knoxbridge Café – if you need refreshment be sure to arrive there before 2 pm. Look left and there is a pub, now re-opened as The Hop Bine Inn.

After Knoxbridge, heading towards Paley Farm

Turn right, cross the former Roman road and left into the footpath that leads just to the right of the electricity poles. Paley Farm is in the distance and according to the Ordnance Survey Explorer Map 136, there are earthworks here, Castle Bank, but little to identify them now.

The path follows the stream closely until, finally, you climb up to the electricity poles to the track on the approach to the farm.

Follow the track round to the right to the waymark on the gate and turn left, 'over' the next gate and cross the field heading towards the cottages, the exit gate is to the right.

Turn left along the lane and look for the path on the right between the last two concrete outhouses. The path is waymarked but, using the fence on the right as a marker, continue straight across the field to the foot bridge, through the hedge, over the stream and follow the line of trees towards Hartridge Manor Cottages. This section is peaceful and walking on grassland next to the stream makes a pleasant change from the hard going of the Thames Path and the towns and cities that have been navigated.

Reaching the fence, turn right and follow the path up to the gate and to the lane beyond. Turn left, past Hartridge Manor Cottages (they were a former corn mill powered by a waterwheel – 'Kent's Millers Tales'), and up the valley through trees towards Hocker Edge. In April, the wood is carpeted with wood anemones lighting up the ground with their white flowers, in May and June the rhododendrons are in flower and in summer the canopy provides a welcome relief to the heat of the Low Weald.

The track descends to pass two houses on the right, Dean House and Folly Hill Cottage, and after 20 metres look for the footpath on the left, waymarked with a stone sign. Walk up through the trees, over the style and, keeping close to the hedge on the right, follow the waymarked path straight ahead, eastwards, up the hill heading for the highest point.

It is a steady climb up to Hocker Edge (348 ft) but at the top you are rewarded with fine views west over the valley and an ideal picnic spot if the weather is good. This is one of the exceptional views of 1066 Harold's Way and a chance to rest awhile with only 2¼ miles to go to Sissinghurst Castle, National Trust and tearooms and a further 1½ miles to the Bus Stop (Arriva: Service 5, Sandhurst to Maidstone)

Walk along the path to join the lane and after almost ½ mile, the gates to Hartridge House are reached. The waymarked footpath is on the left, by the entrance to Staddleden.

Continue through the gate and follow the waymarked signs across the fields. When I walked the path, there were horses in the paddocks and electric fences but the path was clearly defined and safe with 'reminders' to make sure that all the gates were securely closed and 'latched'.

Head diagonally across the field towards the wood framed cottage and continue along the footpath by the bluebell woods to the left. The final stile leads left into the trees and within a few metres, turn right towards the traffic noise of the busy Roman road, the A229.

Look left across the A229 and continue 1066 Harold's Way into London Lane, cross the A229 as there is a wide verge on the other side.

At the junction with Frittenden Road turn right and walk up the hill to the sharp bend at the top. Take care as there can be some traffic on this short stretch of Frittenden Road and it is important to remain visible and safe as unfortunately, there are no footpath alternatives.

At the top of the hill, turn left along the Bridle Path to Sissinghurst Castle. After Horse Race House keep right, then look for the waymarked path on the right by the side of an orchard. Walk parallel to the track along the hedge and we can just begin to see the Castle greenhouses.

Head towards the gate and look to the right for a gap in the hedge and the entrance to the NT Car park. Walk down to the bottom and one of the Castle tearooms can be seen to the left (you do not have to be a member to sample the tearoom delights).

Pick up your feet, you can rest at the estuary, the camp for tonight.

To catch the bus from Sissinghurst Village, leave Sissinghurst Castle by the main drive and at the first corner, where the road turns right, there is a unique National Trust stile on the left that swings down to allow you to cross into the field.

Keep to the hedge on the right and walk down the field until you are abreast with the wood on the right.

Over stile and look down the drive away from the Castle to the entrance to the wood and the permitted path to Sissinghurst village. The path is clearly defined and there are marker posts. Through the wood exiting via a kissing gate and turn left, over a footbridge and up to a tarmac track that leads to the main A262, turn right and continue to the Memorial Ground bus stop.

At The Bull, there is story board that traces the history of Sissinghurst which stands on the line of the old Roman road and, perhaps, the route of Harold and his army. Opposite is Chapel Lane and the next stage of 1066 Harold's Way, Walk 9, Sissinghurst to Bodiam Castle.

For the bus stop, continue along the A262, towards the Memorial Ground. Buses to Staplehurst Station, The Railway Tavern, Staplehurst and Maidstone are on the north side and to Cranbrook, Hawkhurst and Sandhurst on the south side of the road.

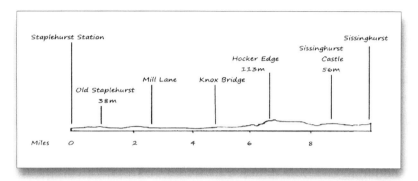

Knox Bridge

Derives from the OE 'cnocc' meaning hillock and relates to the Knockes, recorded as 'dwellers by the hill'. In the 14th century, it became known as 'Knockes Bridge' ('The Place Names of Kent' – Judith Glover).

There is evidence of older earthworks on the path leaving Knox Bridge and on the way to Hartridge, a wooded ridge with a history of watermills.

The following link gives a little more information about Staplehurst Castle Bank (Monument Number 414968):

http://homepage.mac.com/philipdavis/Indexs/EngCounty/Kent.html

and for 'Kent's Millers Tales', visit:

http://www.millarchive.com/kent/cranbrookstale/cranbrookstale.aspx

Sissinghurst and Sissinghurst Castle NT

Sissinghurst village owes its prosperity to the growth of the weaving industry established during the reign of Edward III and which continued into the 16th century. Sissinghurst Castle is the best known of the old wealthy weaver's houses dating from the late 15th century. In 1930, after years of neglect and misuse it was rescued by Sir Harold Nicolson and his wife, the writer Victoria Sackville-West who restored what was left of the once-great manor house and in its grounds established one of the finest and most celebrated gardens in the country. It is now part of the National Trust. (www.nationaltrust.org.uk)

1066 HAROLD'S WAY WALK 9:
SISSINGHURST TO
BODIAM CASTLE ⟨🚶 Public Footpath⟩

Distance: 11 miles
Time: 4½ hours
Maps: OS Explorer: 136,137 & 125

Travel
www.travelinesoutheast.org.uk
Bus
Arriva Service 5:
Maidstone to Sandhurst
via Sissinghurst village
Cross Country Service 349:
Hastings to Hawkhurst
via Bodiam and Sandhurst

Parking
Sissinghurst: On Street
Sandhurst: On Street
Bodiam Castle: NT Car Park*
Bodiam: No Parking**

* NT car parks are time restricted
** There is very little parking around The
Green, the Castle Inn car park is for patrons
only and the gates are closed at National
Trust car parks when visiting times are over.
The Bus is recommended.

Accommodation
Maidstone, Sissinghurst Castle, Cranbrook,
Sandhurst, Hastings & St Leonards
www.1066country.com
Appendix 4: Tourist Information links

Refreshments
Sissinghurst: Convenience store & P.O.
Iden Green: The Woodcock (open Tue to Sun)
www.thewoodcockinn.com

Sandhurst: Johnson's General Store
Sandhurst Tea Rooms (Thu to Sun)
The Swan
Bodiam Castle: NT tearooms
Bodiam: The Castle Inn

Connecting Long Distance Paths
High Weald Landscape Trail
Sussex Border Path
Local Trails
Benenden Village History Trail

Geography
A mix of arable farming, livestock, meadow,
orchards and hopfields that is found in this
part of Wealden Kent along the High Weald
Landscape Trail towards Benenden. A climb
up to the High Weald to follow the Roman
road at Sandhurst that leads to the Kent
Ditch and the Sussex Border Path to Bodiam.
The former Appledore Estuary once filled the
Kent Ditch and the valley behind the Castle
and must have been some sight.

Path Profile & Difficulty
Gentle to more steeply undulating. Moderate
effort.
The path is always close to the line of the
Roman road which can be seen clearly at
Benenden and at Sandhurst. The paths are
clear and well waymarked for the majority of
this section. There are stiles and gates to
negotiate but most are in good repair. There is
only a little road walking and traffic is
minimal, at least at the time I walked this
section.

Reflections

The landscape was so very different in 1066, with heavily wooded hillsides and the tidal estuary extending into the valleys around Bodiam and Sedlescombe – natural hazards to navigate. Once again, Harold's route follows the Roman road that passed through this former heavily wooded region, through Benenden, Sandhurst on the ridge and finally Bodiam. This Roman road is different, green lanes and forgotten sunken tracks, marked by lines of trees, take us straight across country in a clear line. You can look down on the overgrown road and imagine it full of Saxon men, women, horses and wagons, straining, pulling to make headway.

It is a very peaceful walk through a beautiful English landscape of valleys and streams and wooded hills, up and down but not too taxing to finish at perhaps the most beautiful castle in all of England.

There was no Castle in 1066 and the Castle Inn had not yet opened its doors for all-day food. Its garden, stretching down to the River Rother, would have been ideal for a short stop – "6000 pints, some bottles of cider, pies and who wants chips?"

The Walk

Starting at The Bull Inn, cross the road into Chapel Lane opposite and after a few metres turn right at the footpath sign. We will follow this path for ½ mile, 10 minutes, until the drive down to Buckhurst Farm.

A little way along the path is a footpath left, my original route that was close to the line of the Roman road, but the path ended up on a busy road. Now, 1066 Harold's Way continues straight ahead.

The path dips down to the lane and 1066 Harold's Way turns left towards Buckhurst Farm, waymarked as a restricted footpath. Down the hill, over the cattle grid and at the entrance to the farm there is a clear footpath sign left. The stream here, according to the OS map, drains into the splendidly named Lake Chad partly covering the site of a much older mill pond and mill

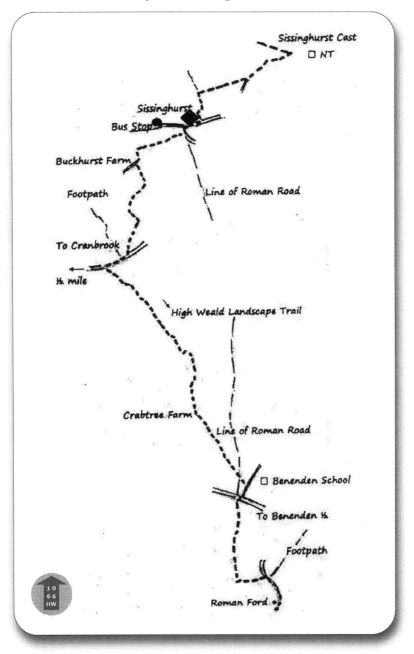

Sissinghurst Cast

□ NT

Sissinghurst

Bus Stop

Buckhurst Farm

Footpath

Line of Roman Road

To Cranbrook

½ mile

High Weald Landscape Trail

Crabtree Farm

Line of Roman Road

□ Benenden School

To Benenden ½

Footpath

Roman Ford

10 66 HW

('Kent's Millers Tales').

Across the field and at the kissing gate turn right to follow the track for almost ¾ mile to the Cranbrook Road. The track twists and turns past an uninhabited grand cottage (the grass has been cut, the garden is tidy but it's empty, very eerie, can I smell gingerbread?). Continue over the bridge and up the hill through woods banked with rhododendrons. Turn right at the road and walk towards Cranbrook, passing the waymark for the High Weald Landscape Trail on the right.

At the Cranbrook sign the Public Footpath post can be seen ahead on the left. Take care this road has no footpath but a reasonable wide verge keeps walkers safe.

Through the gate marked Fir Tree Farm and up the hill, keeping to the Public Footpath to the left of the orchard. Through the kissing gate on the left and continue up and along

Walking the Roman Road near Benenden

the footpath. At the top, bear right across the field and in the distance, on the horizon, is Benenden School.

Through the kissing gate and halfway down the hill, follow the path left through the gate and, keeping the hedge to the right, continue down the hill and follow the waymarks across the field to the steps into the wood.

At the bottom, cross the bridge and walk to the right of the barn and then left, behind the barn, to pick up the waymarked Trail signs on the right. Up the hill to Crabtree Farm and continue through what appears to be a garden (and the home of a very noisy and excitable dog) to pick up the waymarked Trail again towards Benenden School.

Continue through the kissing gate to enter Benenden School parkland, walk up the hill heading for the top right hand corner of the field, through the opening and bear left up to the brow of the hill and the large chestnut trees. Through the gate by the side of the sports field and walk down to the School drive, following the fence on the right. To the left between the trees, there are glimpses of the imposing school buildings.

Turn right towards the School Gates and at the main road, turn right and take the waymarked lane on the left to follow the track of the Roman road once again, to continue down to what is shown on the OS map as a Roman Ford. ('Roman Roads in Britain,' Ivan D Margary).

At this point, the top of Benenden Church is to the east and on the horizon, south, is North's Seat, the highest point above Hastings at 170 metres. For the moment, remain on the High Weald Landscape Trail next to the Roman road although, sometime in the future, I would dearly love to use the Roman road as the route for 1066 Harold's Way.

Through the kissing gates and keep the Roman Road to the right all the way down to Stream Farm. Sadly and despite a search, there does not seem to be any evidence now of the paved ford but of course, I may be looking in the wrong place.

In the valley, look for the gate in the left hand corner, cross the bridge and turn left up the hill along the green lane and turn right along the road into Iden Green.

Walk up the hill into the village and on the left just before the row of houses, is the footpath, the sign is back from the road and can be missed. Follow the clearly marked footpath to an orchard, take a couple of steps into the orchard and look to the right down the hill and just beyond the electricity pole you can see a track that meanders up between the trees. Walk through the orchard, down one of the aisles, to join up with the track that leads to Woodcock Lane and the Woodcock Public House. The Woodcock is well worth a stop either now at this halfway point of Walk 9 or to return to at a later date.

The footpath is to the left of the pub and leads to Standen Street, turn left and after a half mile, there is a sharpish left hand bend with a footpath sign and a fine view over the valley to Sandhurst on your right and a windmill on your left, (with the word Street in the village name it is quite likely that the Roman road is close).

Climb the stile and continue straight ahead, down the field towards the arch in the trees and over the stile. Follow the hedge on the right until the field opens out and then head diagonally right across to the opposite corner – there are waymarks but they may well be hidden by brambles - over the stile, through the trees and walk down the hill past the right hand side of the lake and through the gate. If there is no path marked, head diagonally left across the field and walk up the hill keeping the trees to the left. We are heading for the 'big' tree on the immediate horizon - there are few waymarks and the 'big' tree will act as our guide – to what was once the stile underneath the tree.

Continue ahead, with the hedge to the left, down to and through Lords Wood. Back into daylight and turn right to follow the field around to the end of the trees ahead. At the top, do not take the tempting gate on the right into woodland lane - it is private - the correct footpath is just around the corner. Again head diagonally right across the field, roughly south (the path may or may not be marked through the crops) and Sandhurst

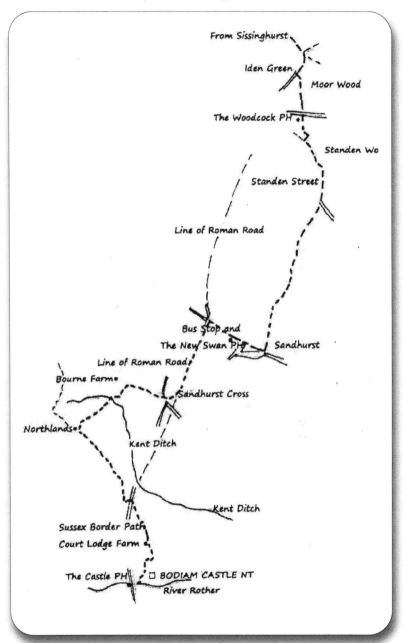

The imposing Bodiam Castle viewed from the south

Windmill comes into view again. Over the stile and bear right up to and in front of the school and walk along to Rye Road and Sandhurst.

Opposite is a Petrol Station and Johnson's of Sandhurst General Store. Turn right, up to the top of the hill, and Rye Road becomes Queen Street and then Sharps Hill.

This last section will take about 1½ hours to walk to Bodiam Castle.

Unless you feel the need to visit The Swan or the tea rooms, stay on the right hand path until the end of the village and the junction with Sponden Lane, (Sponden Lane follows the line of the old Roman Road).

At the junction, cross Queen Street to the south side, by the Farm Shop, and walk a little way left up the lane leading to Bayford House and, by the telephone pole, is the waymarked footpath up over a stile.

The path continues along the line of the Roman Road, across the field, over the stile at the top and, keeping the hedge on the left, walk through fields bordered by old hawthorn hedges. They remind me of my childhood in the fifties before the total advent of progress meant that many of these hedges were destroyed as fields became larger and more productive. It is good to see them again.

The path here is reasonably clear and leads to a stile on the left and a sharp turn right and left to continue the path south. This path has all the hallmarks of a much used Roman road, now it is a ditch bordered by trees, and on a hot day the dappled shade provides some relief.

Continue down to the road, turn right and walk up the hill to Sandhurst Cross and turn right at the crossroads along Silverden Lane for about 50 metres. As the lane bears right carry straight on along Bourne Lane with lovely views over the valley marking the Kent and Sussex border.

As the road takes a sharp left turn and becomes a track, the path carries straight on up to a stile and into a field sown with crops. There should be a marked path but head for the spur and the tree at the top of the hill and then head down towards the Oast Houses of Bourne Farm.

Leave the field over a stile, about 50 metres to the right of the telephone pole in the corner, down the steep slope and across the lane into the field opposite. Walk around the bottom of the field, keeping the hedge and the hop fields on the left until you reach the Kent Ditch in a deep gully to the left. Once the upper reaches of the Appledore Estuary it now marks the line of county border.

Over the bridge and then right, diagonally across the field to the corner and right up the hill, keeping the wood on the right, to a gap in the trees. There is an absence of waymark signs but through the gap and bear left up the track heading for Northlands Farm at the top of the hill to link with the Sussex Border Path to Bodiam Castle.

At the waymark post, turn left along the broad path, down the hill and continue through Lower Northlands Farm to Bodiam Road. There are good views back along the valley and an occasional glimpse of the Kent Ditch to the east of Bodiam Castle – just watch out for rabbit holes along the path, I am sure that the rabbits know where they are but we don't.

At Bodiam Road, turn right and the path is opposite, (the waymark post may be overgrown with ivy) and follow the path diagonally up the hill to the oak tree in the corner, over the stile to follow the waymark to a fence and a further stile. Ahead is a grassy mound and the waymark sign points to the top of the hill leading to the path by the side of the fence and our first glimpse of Bodiam Castle.

Down into the grounds of this beautiful castle rising out of it's wide moat and the grand noble entrance in front, *(the Ticket Office to the right has a display relating to the history of the Castle)*. Continue along the path to the right of the Castle and past the ditch.

To the right, is an indentation that creates a grassy track leading over the hill down towards the castle gate, away from the path. It is believed that this is the route of the Roman Road down to the bridge and the place where Harold would have crossed the river. It is the same Roman road that started in Rochester and will end near Sedlescombe. The raised bank of the present River Rother can be seen in the valley and further on is the track of the Kent and East Sussex Railway.

Looking across at what would have been the tidal valley of the River Rother, there is a wildness about this place even in summer. The 'Anglo-Saxon Chronicles' identified it as the Appledore Estuary and Bodiam is at the western limit where an easy crossing could be made over the old Roman causeway. Perhaps the bridge in front is on the same site as the Roman causeway that funnelled Harold's army together on their urgent march to Caldbec Hill.

On a July afternoon, Bodiam Castle is busy with visitors. If you have the energy, the Castle is well worth a visit, if you haven't, the tearooms or the Castle Inn opposite the Castle entrance provide an opportunity to relax. A visit to the pub, part of which dates back to the 14th century, would be more than appropriate as this area was for around 60 years associated with growing hops for Guinness. Bodiam Station, across the valley, is still in use but the line is not connected to the national rail network at Robertsbridge – a pity, although there are plans to restore and extend the line in the future. The bus stop for the 349 to Hastings or to Hawkhurst is just by the gate. They run every two hours either way but do check times as the last bus is between 5pm and 6pm and the Sunday service is limited.

At this point, the length of the Roman road from London to Bodiam is 58 miles but we have travelled 90 miles with our detours and scenic routes to avoid the traffic and the congestion of modern England.

If you need to return to Staplehurst Station, for rail connections, there is a service from Bodiam Castle to Sandhurst which will drop you off outside The Swan to connect with Arriva Service 5 to Maidstone which will take you to Station Approach.

Alternatively you could always break the walk at Sandhurst and add the remainder to Walk 10.

High Weald Landscape Trail

A 90 mile path from Horsham, West Sussex to Rye, East Sussex passing through an Area of Outstanding Natural Beauty – the High Weald - still the most wooded area of England. The guidebook is regrettably out of print. http://www.kent.gov.uk/leisure-and-culture/explore-kent/walking/high-weald-landscape-trail.htm

Benenden

There is history here from Roman times.

Benenden lies on our Roman road and was mentioned in the Doomsday book. The village is worth a visit with cricket on The Green in summer and a pub to relax at but it is away from 1066 Harold's Way. Visit the village website for history trails to download: www.benendenvillage.org.uk/trails/Benendentrails2.pdf & www.benendenvillage.org.uk/

Benenden School

Formerly Hemstead House and Park, the school, founded in 1924, is one of the foremost girls boarding schools in the country although there has been a house on the site since before the 15th century. There is a fascinating history of both the house and school at:www.benenden.kent.sch.uk/benenden%20community/SchoolHistory

Sandhurst

The present day Sandhurst Cross, south of Sandhurst, lies on the route of the old Roman road that we have been following from Maidstone and Rochester and it ends at Beauport Park, near Hastings. Before the coastline changed, Sandhurst Cross would have overlooked the Appledore Estuary. As the ridgeway to Rye increased in importance it is likely that Sandhurst developed along the Rye road to take advantage of the increased traffic and away from the church and the Roman road. www.villagenet.co.uk/esussex-iron/villages/sandhurst.php

Sussex Border Path

This 150 miles long path follows the inland boundary of both East and West Sussex, from Thorney Island in the west to Rye in the east. www.sussexborderpath.co.uk/

Bodiam Castle NT

There are few more beautiful castles in England. It almost seems to float on the water of the moat. Bodiam was at the limit of the navigable River Rother and following French attacks on both Rye and Winchelsea, Richard II gave permission for a castle to be built to defend against further French attacks. By the time that the castle was completed in 1385, we had re-gained control of the Channel and the Castle never saw action until 1645 when it was partially destroyed by Parliamentary troops during the Civil War. The castle fell into decay until rescued by Lord Curzon of Kedleston who, in 1925, bequeathed it to the nation. Today, there is a continuing programme of restoration and repair for this the last great medieval military fortress built. (www.nationaltrust.org.uk)

The Castle Inn, Bodiam

Opposite the castle is the Castle Inn. Formerly known as the Red Lion it was rebuilt and renamed in 1885 but its roots go back to the 15th century when merchants and tradesmen would have come on business to the castle. Later, it provided accommodation for visitors to the romantic Castle ruins and for the barges on the River Rother. It was known as 'a picturesque brick and tile hung pub with a cosy tap room warmed by an open hearth with andirons upon which logs burned in winter and around which were high backed settles'(Arthur Mee's 'Kent'). Today, it is still welcoming with a range of well kept Shepherd Neame beers and a good selection of food. The beer garden is a relief after the walk from Sissinghurst, with views south over the flood plain and in the summer's haze, you can almost imagine the shimmer of water.

http://www.shepherd-neame.co.uk/pubs/pubs.php/castleinn_robertsbridge

The Bodiam Ferry Company

The River Rother remained navigable for barges from Rye until the 19th century but trade declined when the railway was built - read the story board by the River at Bodiam Castle. You can still cruise the River Rother from Newenden. www.bodiam-ferry.co.uk/

Kent & East Sussex Railway

The line opened at the beginning of the 20thcentury and linked Tenterden with Robertsbridge and the mainline to London and in 1905, it was extended to Headcorn. After 1945, the line declined in popularity and was finally closed in the 1960's with the last of the 'Hop Pickers Specials'. The K&ESR is now run by volunteers, with services between Tenterden and Bodiam Castle. http://www.kesr.org.uk/

Hops

Hops have been grown in the Rother Valley for over four hundred years. Used first as a preservative, they gave beer a bitterness and an individual and distinctive flavour. Arthur Guinness & Son acquired several farms around Bodiam Station in the early 20th century and the area became a major hop growing centre. The Kent and East Sussex

Railway gave ready access to the national rail network enabling the hops to be easily transported. At their peak in September, the K&ESR carried over 4000 hop-pickers, mainly women and children, who saw the few weeks of hop picking as their annual holiday.

Special trains operated from London Bridge to Robertsbridge bringing 'hoppers' from London to Bodiam. 'Hoppers friends' trains ran each weekend during the picking season bringing husbands and fathers to visit their families. The most obvious reminders of the once thriving industry are the circular Oast Houses. Guinness sold the last of their farms in 1976 as the brewing industry changed, due to amalgamation, more efficient methods for brewing beer and the increased demand for lager, finally resulting in the closure of the Park Royal brewery in 2005.

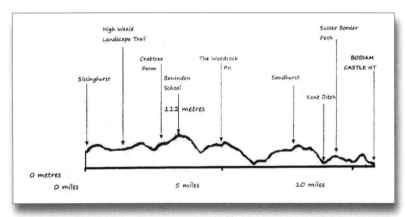

Originally, my plan had been to follow the Roman road as far as the footpath would allow from Sissinghurst. The OS map shows the remains of the Roman road and indeed you can see evidence of an old road, guarded by the trees but it is not fully a public footpath. That route leads to the busy Benenden Road which is not really a safe option and as a result 1066 Harold's Way follows the alternative route along the High Weald Landscape Trail.

We are so close to being able to walk where the Romans and Harold marched that it is a pity that the old Roman road cannot be re-opened for 1066 Harold's Way and your support may help. Visit www.1066haroldsway.co.uk and use the e-mail contact to register your views on the Roman road.

123

1066 HAROLD'S WAY WALK 10:
BODIAM TO BATTLE VIA SEDLESCOMBE

Public Footpath

Distance: 9.25 miles
Time: 3½ hours
Maps: OS Explorer 136 & 124

Travel: www.travelinesoutheast.org.uk
www.nationalrail.co.uk
Bus:
Stagecoach Service 349
Hastings to Hawkhurst via Bodiam
Stagecoach Service 304/5
Hastings to Tunbridge Wells via Battle
Rail
South Eastern: Battle Station
(London to Hastings)
www.southeasternrailway.co.uk
Parking
Bodiam: No Parking**
Bodiam Castle: NT Pay *
Sedlescombe: Car Park & On Street
Battle: Pay and Display
Battle Abbey: EH Pay*

* NT & EH car parks are time restricted
** There is very little parking around The
Green, the Castle Inn car park is for patrons
only and the gates are closed at National
Trust car parks when visiting times are over.
The Bus is recommended.

Accommodation (Appendix 4)
Tourist Information: Battle, Sedlescombe,
St Leonards and Hastings
www.1066country.com

Refreshments
Bodiam: The Castle Inn
Bodiam Castle NT

Sedlescombe: The Queens Head
The Brickwall Hotel
Kester House B&B
Village Stores
Battle: Shops and pubs
Abbey Hotel (SN)
Battle Abbey Restaurant EH

Connecting Long Distance Paths
Sussex Border Path
1066 Country Walk

Difficulty
Moderate
There is one reasonable climb on this section
but most ascents are more gradual.
In early spring, many of the pastures can have
sheep with lambs or cows with calves and
appropriate care should be taken. Footpaths
are well defined but are not always
waymarked and some stiles are in poor
condition.
There is only a little road walking along
country lanes and traffic is minimal.
Path Profile & Geography
This section is over the lower hills of the High
Weald between the valleys of the Rivers
Rother and Brede and up to Battle walking
mostly on Public Footpaths.
It is a mix of undulating arable farm land,
livestock, meadow and woodland with some
stiles and gates. Join the B2244 through
Sedlescombe to briefly follow the Roman road
and Harold's route of 1066.

And this valley was once all water - looking over
the River Brede towards Hastings

Reflections

Perhaps there was a shimmer on this inland sea and an early
morning mist rising into the trees. Eastwards, the Appledore
Estuary seemed to spread as far as the eye could see as the sun
began to rise in the sky. It was a wild and desolate place and no
doubt a strong breeze was already pulling at the water as men
and horses prepared for the final few miles to Caldbec Hill.
South the old Roman road drew the eyes up the hill between
the trees of the forest, an arrow pointing towards the imminent
battle.

This walk is a collection of images and a last glance at the
Castle and if we are lucky, it will seem to rise out of its moat in
an early morning ghostly thrall. Guinness fields and steam
trains, the 'Hoppickers Specials', charcoal burners clearing
forest greens to practise ancient arts turning wood into
charcoal, smoke drifting lazily upwards through the trees. In

the valley is a squat towered stone church set against a backdrop of trees. It is such a beautiful setting to look down on, sitting on the hilltop green bench, that it is worthy of a small prayer before the walk to the gates of Battle Abbey to finally pay our tribute to Harold II, King of England, who gave meaning to 1066 Harold's Way.

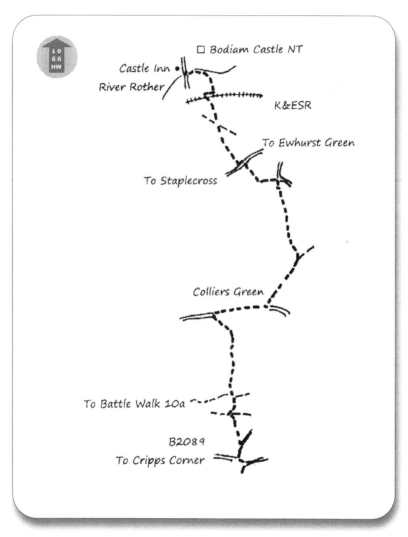

The Walk

The country bus stops at the gate to Bodiam Castle. Walk down the road, south, towards the bridge over the River Rother. Close to the bridge are story boards recounting history that starts with the Romans who built a dock to transport their iron. It is quite likely that the quay and the causeway would still have been there in Saxon times.

Looking at this landscape, it is hard to believe that the River Rother was once the tidal Appledore Estuary flowing out to sea at Rye. The sea would have covered the valley eastwards and, in the 14th and 15th centuries, it was wide enough and deep enough for the biggest ships of medieval England to be built at Appledore and Smallhythe. Today, where there was once a wide tidal channel there are now fields and the Kent Ditch and just enough water for pleasure cruises from Northiam to Bodiam.

Cross the bridge and climb the stile on the left to follow the Sussex Border Path along the top of the flood bank by the River Rother. Just before the gate turn right towards the Kent and East Sussex Railway line, keeping the ditch to your left. This area was once owned by Guinness and given over to hop growing – in summer, the railway carried the hop pickers to the farms and transported the hops back to the brewery – the line was closed in 1961. The farms have long been sold.

When you reach the Kent & East Sussex Railway (K&ESR) railway line turn right and walk by the fence until you reach the crossing point over the railway. Looking back towards the Castle you get some idea of the width of the River Rother where Harold crossed in 1066. Instead of a bridge, which was expensive and difficult to build, the Romans tended to build up the river bed with rocks to create a ford, perhaps where the present bridge is now.

Over the railway line and follow the path behind the barn with the hedge on your right, across the bridge and walk along the bottom of the field heading due south, towards the houses on the horizon. Across the next bridge and up the field, following the line of the electricity poles and keeping the fence on your left. The path to Ewhurst Green branches to the left but we continue up the hill to the stile in the top corner of the field and along the green lane to the road.

Turn left and the footpath is just past the white clapperboard house. Over the stile and follow the clear path through meadows and a spinney to a small drive and turn right. In late May and June, these meadows are filled with a glorious display of wild flowers to brighten any day's walk.

After about 30 metres turn left through a gate, along the drive for a few steps and the stile is on the right. The path keeps to the right hand fence, down to the corner of the field to follow the waymarks, through a garden and across the bridge. Either walk straight across the field, if a path has been marked through

There is a church hidden deep in the valley, amongst the trees ...

crops, or follow the side of the field left for about a 100 metres to a waymarked bridge, it is just after the gap/gateway in the hedge, and into a large field that climbs up away from us.

The horizon curves above and initially, you should aim for the top of the curve in the centre of the field - there should be a clear path through the crops. At the brow of the hill, the immediate destination becomes easier to spot. Look ahead, south, to the next ridge and walk towards the gap in the trees on the horizon. If there are crops, it is difficult to keep your bearing unless the path is clearly marked by the farmer. As you climb look back and the white house should be directly in front of the brick house higher up the valley, if it is, you are on the right track.

To the right of the top of the field is a stile. Into the next field and keeping the pond to your left continue up the hill, next to the hedge until you reach a small bridge left. Cross, turn right and continue with the hedge on the right until the waymarks point diagonally across the field towards the houses in front and Colliers Green.

The Saxon Times

Caldbec Hill   13th October 1066

Late extra: 13th October 1066 Nightfall

Tomorrow will decide the future of England.
This battle will be remembered for ever in our history.

Keep the line and we will win
Keep the line and we will win
Keep the line and we will win

The second army arrives later,
Battle hardened and experienced.
They will ensure the tide is turned
In our favour, in our favour.

Hold the line and we will win
Hold the line and we will win
Hold the line and we will win

May God speed and save us all tomorrow

Long Live King Harold
Long Live King Harold
Long Live King Harold

This area would have been heavily wooded and part of the great forest of the Weald. The charcoal produced around the Weald supported the local iron industry, much prized by the Romans and was the main reason for the Roman road to be built south from Maidstone, the road that has guided this walk.

At the corner of the field is a stile leading into a drive, bear left and at the main road turn right, and after about a ½ mile, look for the stile by the gate on the opposite side of the road - take care, there is no waymark.

Down the green lane, through paddocks and head for the telegraph pole in the middle of the field on which there is the waymark sign pointing towards the corner, through the gate and into the wood - bear right and after a few metres, the path opens out.

Up the hill towards Ewhurst Green

Looking back towards Streetfield and Brede High Woods –
the modern Andreasweald.

Halfway up the hill is a stile on the right. Turn left and follow the waymarks up and over the hill towards Miles Farm.

Bear right up the grass lane to the stile, and walk down the hill to the gate at the bottom keeping the fence to your left and on into Ellenwhorne Lane.

Turn right and at the T junction turn left and look for the footpath, on the right, through Brede High Wood (the footpath is the second entrance to the wood).

Walk down the path to the cross-paths and turn right, following the waymarks, and after 30 metres, turn left and here, standing still in front of me, was a fox, watching, waiting, thinking before it decided it had better things to do and more places to see.

This mixed wood, full of the sound of wildlife, dappled shade, streams and tracks, now part of the Woodland Trust, is perhaps the kind of forest that grew at the time of Harold. Would he have been impressed by the solitude of the wood or too nervous about what lay ahead?

Continue along the clear path to the edge of the wood and up the field, probably the stiffest climb of this section of 1066 Harold's Way. At the footpath sign bear left and continue with the hedge on your right through the swing gate at the top leading into Hurst Lane. The footpath is directly opposite with a typical East Sussex stone footpath marker set low down into the ground.

Keep to the path, ignoring any tracks into the wood on the right, and exit into a lane, turn right. The road bears left and the waymark directs you into the field ahead with a bench and a glorious view over the wooded Brede valley to Battle on the horizon. In good weather it is an ideal spot to drink in this Wealden view before the final climb to Battle.

The valley below was once part of the Appledore Estuary, full of water and only to be crossed by ferry. This wide tidal river valley, that met the sea at Rye, would have taken Harold's Army some time to cross. It gives rise to the possibility that the bulk of Harold's army took the high road through Cripps Corner and Vine Hall to the rendezvous at Caldbec Hill.

Keep the hedge on your left and ignore any footpaths off to the left. You are now on the final approach to Sedlescombe. Down the hill, into the lane and take the left hand fork, along the unmade track, into the village.

The line of the old Roman road reputedly follows the main road down towards the bridge over the River Brede and the old buildings that line the old Roman road reflect Sedlescombe's earlier importance (see panel). On the Green stand the Brickwall Hotel, the Queens Head Inn and the Village Stores. The bus stop for the bus into Hastings is further down the Green.

Walk down The Green to the Bridge Garage and at the sign showing 'The Antique Collector's Market' turn right down a lane towards a tennis court and continue by the side of the children's playground. Cross the bridge and turn immediately right. Continue along the clear path by the side of a stream for a ½ mile and aim for the gate to the left of the house ahead and the busy A21 - the main London to Hastings road. The footpath to Battle is directly opposite over the stile.

The fields through which we are walking, either side of the A21, would once have been under water. The grasses and reeds still show evidence of occasional flooding in what was once the upper reaches of the old Appledore Estuary of Roman and Saxon times.

We walk alongside the curiously named Felon Wood, following the footpath over the stile, through the trees, into the next meadow and head for the top left hand corner. Turn right along the path and continue over the bridge to Marley Lane, opposite the entrance to Marwin Farm.

Turn left along the road for ¼ mile until a sharp bend and on the right, there is a stile by the gate to Greenwood Yard Cottage – the footpath sign is missing. Continue ahead, keeping to the fence, to a stile and turn left. Unless there is a clear path through the crops, follow the field round the edge to a gap in the hedge at the top of the field and turn right.

Again, follow the edge of the field round, firstly in line with the electricity poles and then left up to the ridge towards Coarsebarn Farm. At the top, turn right, due west, keeping Coarsebarn Farm to the left.

At the gate, look back across the valley towards Sedlescombe. This area is still heavily wooded with gentle rolling hills and you can imagine how this flooded valley looked at the time of Harold with the ripples of the water seen through the trees.

On cue and to shatter the image, a train rattles past on its way from London Charing Cross to Hastings and a picture of Harold in First Class surfaces – not too good an image as Battle Station would have been in the heart of William's camp.

Turn right along the lane and over the railway bridge towards Battle. As the path opens up on the left-hand side, look over the valley to Battle Church and Battle Abbey and Harold's destination. To the left of the church stands Telham Hill where William's army camped prior to the battle. After almost ½ mile, look for the footpath sign on the left, by the Caravan Club Certified Location and opposite a cottage ('The White House'), and follow the path to Caldbec Hill, the meeting point for Harold's army.

Battle is now straight ahead of us but for Harold, there would have been no time to savour the view, Battle as a place did not exist. Walk through the gate at the end of the field past the allotments on our left. At the time of my walk there was a wonderful display of scarecrows but not one of Harold or William – there is a 'Battle Scarecrow Festival' in July.

Continue into the main Battle town car park. In the diagonal corner there is a path to the High Street. Turn left and walk down High Street towards Battle Abbey with a major new exhibition that brings the battle to life and an audio guide to help you walk the battle site.

The railway station, to London, St Leonards and Hastings, is ½ mile south and the bus stop for Hastings is opposite Battle Abbey, outside the Abbey Hotel.

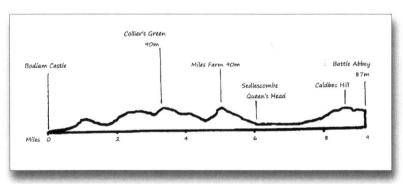

Colliers Green.

This curious name, far from the coalfields of Kent and the North, most likely relates to an association with the family of Robert le Coleyere, around 1240 and later William Collier 1348, and linked to the manufacture of charcoal. The 'Colliers' provided the charcoal for smelting iron ore with the forests of Andreasweald providing the raw material.

I like the story that when an area of woodland was cleared by the charcoal burners and when they moved on, they left a 'green' which was then 'settled' hence Colliers Green.

Sedlescombe.

It was recorded in the Domesday Book but already had a history. You can still follow the line of the Roman road down the main street by the village green to the bridge over the River Brede, once part of the Appledore Estuary and a Roman dock.

The evidence of the prosperity of the village can be seen in the half timbered houses lining the street with many dating back to the 15th century and including the Queen's Head Inn, although much of it is restored.

Up until the Industrial Revolution, Sedlescombe was an important centre for the Sussex iron industry. Iron had been made here since before Roman times and the Roman road was built to link the various Wealden iron-workings to Bodiam and north to London. It is believed that this Roman road was 'metalled' using slag from the iron workings which produced a very heavy duty road.

As iron production declined, new industry was sought. The gunpowder ground by the local water mills was reputedly the best in Europe but after an explosion in December 1764, when four men died, there was a certain reluctance from the rest of the workers to continue production. The mill was behind Bridge Garage.

In 1867, a large hoard of some 3,000 coins dating from King Edward the Confessor's reign (1042-1066), were found in Sedlescombe, reputedly buried by Harold's paymaster after the Battle of Hastings. www.sedlescombe.org.uk/ sedlescombe.east-sussex.co.uk/

There is a curious lead water pump in the centre of The Green and I am surprised that the village population survived the lead poisoning. (The lead is actually a veneer. 'Sedlescombe's Pump and Pumphouse – a brief history' by Pauline J Raymond. Sedlescombe Parish Council, available from the Village Stores).

www.sedlescombe.org.uk/An/History/QuizAnswers.pdf. has an interesting village quiz.

Beauport Park nr Hastings.

The Roman Iron Industry started around here immediately after the Roman invasion in AD43. It lasted until the mid 3rd century when the ore and fuel resources were considerably depleted. The scale was enormous with an estimated 50,000 tons of slag deposited around the site ('The Kent and Sussex Weald': Brandon). A road was created to Maidstone, docks built at Sedlescombe and a fleet base at Bodiam to transport either the pig iron and/or the ore. The remains of a Bath House in the woods at Beauport Park suggest that the needs of the Romans were not forgotten in this outpost of the Empire.

Walk 10a

Bodiam Castle to Battle Abbey, via Cripps Corner follows the old ridgeways that would have been the probable route for the bulk of Harold's army. This alternative route avoided the Appledore Estuary at Sedlescombe and the walk is available to download from www.1066haroldsway.co.uk

1066 HAROLD'S WAY:
BATTLE AND BATTLE
WALKS ⏵ Public Footpath ⏵

Maps: OS Explorer: 124

Travel: www.travelinesoutheast.org.uk
www.nationalrail.co.uk
Rail:
South Eastern: Battle
(London to Hastings)
www.southeasternrailway.co.uk
Bus
Stagecoach Service 304/5
Hastings to Tunbridge Wells, via Battle
Parking
Battle: Pay and Display
Battle Abbey (EH): Pay (time limited)

Connecting Long Distance Paths
1066 Country Walk

Local Paths
Battle Walk   ESCC Route 21
Download at:www.eastsussex.gov.uk

Accommodation
Battle, Hastings and St Leonards on Sea
See Appendix 4

Refreshments
Battle Abbey (EH): Restaurant
Battle: Many and varied

Tourist Information Centres
Hastings
Queens Square, Priory Meadow, Hastings
Tel: 01424 781111
e-mail: hic_info@hastings.gov.uk
Battle and Bexhill
Battle Abbey, Gatehouse, Battle
TN33 0AD
Tel: 01424 773721
e-mail: battletic@rother.gov.uk

Other Weblinks
www.battle-sussex.co.uk

Let battle commence

On 28 September, 1066 with a favourable wind, William landed
unopposed at Pevensey and within a few days had made camp
at Hastings, a few miles along the coast.

Hastings was already partly under the control of the Abbey
of Fecamp in Normandy and welcomed William with open
arms. After William's victory, Hastings was saved the fate of
neighbouring Bexhill and most of the surrounding countryside
that had remained staunchly Saxon.

William now needed to move away from Hastings if he was to
take the Crown of England but there were difficulties. Sussex
was always an inaccessible place.

The Saxon Times

Caldbec Hill   **Sports Report**   **13th October 1066**

Match Preview
By your Sports Correspondent

Think of Harold tomorrow, Saturday, 14th October 1066.

An early kick-off is anticipated and extra time to be played, Saxons against the Normans and their two captains, Harold II and William.

These are the top two teams in this season's league with the Danes, Norwegians and Northumbrians already relegated.

The Saxon defence has been in good form and their proven power attack has seen them to two previous victories.

Although the Normans had not travelled well, they had travelled with hope and did have the advantage of being able to call upon their Cavalry in attack.

The Saxon team, nicknamed 'The Warriors', believe that the strength of the crowd will be a telling point and in a press release issued earlier today, urged all Saxons to come and support them in battle. A close contest is expected for this final premier league game of the season and the Crown will be awarded to the victor.

The result will soon be known and it will give us some idea as to what will happen next season.

It was heavily wooded (the vast Forest of Anderida), the terrain was difficult with high ridges running east to west and the great tidal estuaries isolating Hastings. The ridges had always been seen as safer tracks, even before the Romans, and they supplemented the key Roman roads that ran north to south. The area around Telham, Senlac and Caldbec Hills was an important and strategic crossroads in 1066.

It was vital that William gained control of this key position if he was to break out of his beachhead at Hastings and march on London.

Harold, however, needed to contain William in Hastings behind the barrier of the Ridge, the Appledore Estuary, the Andreasweald and the Sea, natural defences he could use to his advantage. The call went out for 'all Saxon fighting men to meet at the 'Hoar Apple Tree' on Caldbec Hill', a local landmark that marked the crossroads on the Ridge and was well known to Saxons throughout Wessex.

Caldbec Hill would be a natural rendezvous for the Saxon Army, close to Senlac Hill if that was to be chosen as the battle site.

Harold's father, Earl Godwin, owned much of Sussex and it passed to Harold on his death. His land would help provide the extra but untrained men that Harold needed to boost his Army with the added motivation that they would be fighting for their homes. The devastation and retribution that the Saxons would suffer, if they lost, was almost forgotten.

The journey that is 1066 Harold's Way, has traversed the Saxon land of the Andreasweald, following old Roman roads from Westminster to Bodiam and on to Calbec Hill.

It is the final leg of the historic march that first took Harold to Stamford Bridge, back to London and on to Battle.

The Battle of Hastings, 14th October, 1066.

The details are well known. Harold's army was already in formation on the ridge at Senlac Hill. They stood 10 or 12 ranks deep. They had the high ground protected by a steep slope to the north and by streams and hollows on the flank.

William's army had camped around Telham Hill. Early in the morning, they moved north towards Senlac but the bottom of the ridge was marshy and there was only a narrow strip of firm land in the centre through which William could send his troops to line up at the foot of the hill.

The battle began, first, Norman archers moved forward and fired. The English shield wall held firm and the Normans suffered losses when fire was returned. The Norman infantry were next but they were cut down in hand to hand fighting by the fearsome two-handed battle axes of the Saxons. The cavalry, attacking uphill, were ineffective.

Keep the line. Keep the line. Keep the line.

Wave after wave attacked the hill but, with causalities on both sides, the Saxon line still held. They kept the high ground and their position was proving unassailable.

Later as the cavalry pulled back again, the untrained Saxon recruits chased after them believing the battle was won. The Norman line began to give. Some of the troops fled and there was a rumour in the Norman camp that William was dead. William lifted his helmet to rally his men and attacked again with relentless pressure on the Saxon line.

The same tactic of feigned withdrawal lured more of the Saxons down the hill to their death and William ordered an all-out assault. Norman archers shot high in the sky, the infantry attacked the flanks and the Saxon shield wall, reduced by losses, gave.

The regular Saxon soldiers, Housecarls and Thegns, defended Harold but when the Normans fought through they found Harold fallen and wounded and his brothers, Gyrth and Leofwine, dead. If you prefer, Harold was shot in the eye by an arrow, but the likelihood is that he was savagely killed by Norman knights and Harold's Standards, the Fighting Man and the Dragon, captured and sent to the Pope in Rome.

Looking at the evidence of the Bayeux Tapestry, it once seemed, that Harold had been killed by an arrow in the eye but after further examination experts believe that Harold was beheaded and his legs hacked off as a warning to the Saxon people .

Saxon lands were devastated and reprisals were severe against any who stood in William's way as he and his army moved on London and on Christmas Day 1066, William was crowned King in Westminster Abbey.

All that remained of the battle was 'The Malfosse'. The rest is history.

The Malfosse Incident

There is little evidence, some say, that confirms or denies the "The Malfosse" except legend. The Bayeux Tapestry is believed to show that after the Battle of Hastings, the 'victorious' Norman army suffered a great disaster.

The vengeful Normans had gained control of Senlac Hill against a regular Saxon army that had protected Harold with immense courage, fighting to the death. No quarter was spared. However, with the Saxon shield wall finally disintegrating, smaller but still brutal battles for personal survival developed.

The Saxon Times

Somewhere in the Andreasweald.   **Final Battle Edition**   14th October 1066

From your War Correspondent.

Exclusive Eye Witness Report.

They were like dogs after a hare

Once they got the scent

There was no stopping them

Down the hill they ran

Faster

And faster.

They thought that they had won.

They thought that they were proper soldiers

But they just didn't listen.

We could see what would happen

From the top of the hill.

We knew what would happen

At the bottom.

They gave William the upper hand

As we fell back to defend the King.

Runners told us the Second Army was close

But the King was hit

His brothers too

And the word was given.

Fall Back,

Fall Back,

To the Andreasweald,

To the Malfosse.

It's late. It's dusk.

The Second Army's here. At last.

We join the line they've formed

At Malfosse, at Malfosse we whisper.

It's darker now

And on the Normans come

The sound of horses and cries in French

Louder, Louder. Closer, Closer

They are the dogs now after the hare

They have the scent of blood.

We are stronger now and we stand defiant.

We urge the Normans on

For we can win here

For we can win

For we have Malfosse!

And win we did.

In the name of Harold and Saxon England.

Horses and Normans piled high in the ditch. The

ditch that was Malfosse.

And then we disappeared,

Into the night,

Into the Andreasweald.

Remember Malfosse,

A victory, but a hollow one,

For we have lost our King.

For we have lost our country

May God Speed and Save us All from

Norman Rule.

As dusk fell, those still alive fled into the dense Forest of Andreasweald. Overwhelmed and without re-inforcements, the ordinary and conscripted soldiers had just had enough.

Back to October 11th and Harold left London in a hurry without the full complement of his regular army. They had needed additional time to recover from the long march south from Stamford Bridge.

Harold's army for the Battle was made up from those regular soldiers who had marched with him from London and of Wessex men, conscripted and enlisted on the march to Caldbec Hill.

The intention was for the re-enforcements to follow and arrive in time for battle but we know that they arrived too late to help. However, this late arrival presented an opportunity to inflict greater casualties on the Norman army and a lasting and bitter blow to William – 'The Malfosse'.

The Saxon reinforcements, perhaps led by the Earls Edwin, Morcar or Waltheof, set up a new defensive line in front of the Andreasweald and called upon the fleeing soldiers to join them. In front of them lay the many hidden gullies and ditches that were a feature of the terrain.

In the near-dark, the Norman cavalry, engorged and enraged by battle, pursued the fleeing Saxons north over unfamiliar ground. It was too good an opportunity to miss and the Saxons lured and taunted the Norman horsemen onward towards them and the ditch.

In a scene reminiscent of the Charge of the Light Brigade, the Norman horsemen rode faster, over land they did not know, recklessly pursuing the fleeing Saxons and over the edge of the ditch, somersaulting headlong into what became a mass of broken bodies of men and their horses, screaming and dying. Legend has it that they "almost levelled the ravine" and any survivors were killed, no quarter given.

After this final skirmish and victory, the Saxons melted back into the forest, back to their villages leaving the Norman dead behind for William to find.

Some went further afield to what became Wales and Cornwall. It may be that many of the surviving Thegns and Housecarls travelled further away from Norman injustice to Scotland, Ireland or sailed abroad as mercenaries to become known, later, as "The English Guard" in 11thcentury Byzantium.

Battle Abbey

William promised that if God gave him victory he would build a church on the site of the battle. The high altar is said to mark the spot where Harold fell. At the same time as the church was built, the site was renamed 'Battle'.

The Benedictines later built an abbey, dissolved by Henry VIII in 1538 but of William's church there is nothing left and the Abbey has had a chequered history. Much of Battle Abbey was pulled down after The Dissolution and converted into a private house.

The refectory still stands, roofless, but well preserved and the impressive 14thcentury gateway has survived largely in its original state

The house is now a school, and the remaining grounds and buildings are English Heritage. There is a Visitor Centre on site and an excellent café/restaurant provides a fitting end to Harold's Way.

Battle Town

The village of Battle did not exist before the battle. The Battle of Senlac or the Battle of Red Lake later became known as the Battle of Hastings. Today Caldbec Hill, Harold's rendezvous point is crowned by a windmill, east of the A2100, on the road to Whatlington. The town is still dominated by the massive Abbey gatehouse and there are many old buildings, dating back from the 13th century. St Mary's was restored in 1869 but dates in part from the 14th and 15th centuries. Battle Historical Society's Museum, in High Street is also worth a visit.

http://www.sussexmuseums.co.uk/battle.htm

Battle Abbey from the crest of Caldbec Hill, where William of Normandy drew up his army before launching his attack on the English.

Battle Walks

The best place to imagine what the battle must have been like is to stand on the Abbey terrace (Senlac Hill) where the English took up their positions, overlooking the deep gully to the left. Looking south east, there is the low hill rising up to William's camp at Telham Hill. William's Army was drawn up on the Hastings Road on this low hill.

There are many walks and walk guides that cover this historic battle site and it would seem churlish to publish yet another. I have identified some of the walks that I have enjoyed with a short summary of their content, a reference to the author and publication and any link to the website.

At some stage in the future, I do intend to identify a longer route that will join the Senlac, Caldbec and Telham Hills, Malfosse and include key Saxon landmarks in a circular walk of around twelve to fifteen miles. This walk will be available from my website www.1066haroldsway.co.uk and will be free to download.

English Heritage: Battlefield Walk.
Accesses the Battlefield site from within the Abbey, long and short walks. Details available on entry to Battle Abbey.

Battlefield Walks Kent and Sussex: Hastings 1066.   **3¾ miles**
Starting at the Station, the walk follows the battlefield without the need for entry to Battle Abbey, climbs Caldbec Hill and returns to the station. Some road walking involved. Author: Rupert Matthews

Walks into History, Battle Abbey and the Battle of Hastings 1066.   **6½ miles**
Starting at the Pay and Display Car Park, the route skirts the battle site to the west and then covers an area north west of Battle, Saxon land and the edge of the Andreasweald close to Malfosse and back over Caldbec Hill. Author: John Wilks

That Deserved Evil Ditch: The 1066 Malfosse Walk.   **4¾ miles**
Skirts the Battlefield to the west and then takes you north towards Malfosse before returning to the Abbey by Caldbec Hill and Red Lake. Compiled by Neil Clephane-Cameron, Joanne Lawrence and David Sawyer.
Published by Battle and District Historical Society, ISBN 1903099005.

50 Walks in Sussex: Battle, Britain's most famous battlefield.   **6 miles**
Starting at the Pay and Display Car Park, the route descends into the valley behind Senlac Hill and joins 1066 Harold's Way into Sedlescombe. The walk returns along a spur of the 1066 Country Walk through Battle Great Wood to join the main 1066 Country Walk up the hill to Battle. www.theAA.com

East Sussex CC: Battle Walk Route 21.   **4½ miles**
Starting at Battle Station, it climbs up towards Telham Hill before entering Battle Great Wood, crossing the route of the 1066 Country Walk and back to the station.
http://maps.eastsussex.gov.uk/pathstoprosperity/WalkDetail.aspx?walkid=69

1066 HAROLD'S WAY:
EPILOGUE

After the Battle

Harold's body was found by his Danish-law wife, Edith Swan-neck, who was able to recognise Harold from 'marks' that only she knew herself! After Harold's body was identified, there were conflicting accounts of what followed next.

One Norman account relates of burial by the sea – it recounts of William's rage 'He guarded the coast when he was alive and can continue now he is dead'. There was a suggestion that he was buried in sand up to his neck, facing the sea, but a grave washed by sea would have been a noble tomb for a Saxon martyr.

Statue of Edith Swanneck and Harold in West St Leonards Gardens although, from certain angles, she does appear to be strangling poor Harold!

Taken from the mural in
Hastings Town Centre

Another account says that after much pleading by Edith, she was allowed to 'rescue' the body and take it home to Bosham, to be buried by the coast amongst family.

Other stories suggest that some six years later Harold's body was re-buried at Waltham Abbey, a church he re-founded in 1060 and visited and prayed at prior to the Battle of Hastings in September 1066. There are stone inscriptions there that purport to support this view but nobody to date can be really sure where his final resting place is.

Wherever he lies, his final journeys will give the opportunity to create another good walk.

1066 Harold's Way The Final Journey
Walk 1: Hastings to Bosham
Walk 2: Bosham to Waltham Abbey

1066 William's Way
As regards to William, victorious in battle, he now had to claim his throne. His journey took him along the coast to Dover, to Canterbury and then a great sweep around the south of London to enter the City from the north. He was crowned King of England on Christmas Day 1066, at Westminster Abbey.

This tortuous journey to his coronation will form the route of 1066 William's Way and will complete the full circle of the events that surround the Battle of Senlac Hill.

1066 HAROLD'S WAY APPENDIX 1:
WALKING NOTES

What to Wear

1066 Harold's Way is not a particularly demanding walk. It is less challenging than say the South Downs Way or the Pennine Way.

There are no steep climbs up rocky hillsides, weaving in and out of tumbling streams or walking on rough land more suitable for sheep. There is no coarse gorse or heather to scratch unwary legs or sodden peat moors to sap your strength.

The exhilaration is still the same. From the top of the North Downs, you can look out over old battlefields along the River Medway. You can walk along ancient Roman roads that can still be traced on maps. On the Thames Path, there is history at every turn.

As with all walks, you will still need to make proper preparations. The first two sections leaving London are mostly on hard paths, hard on the feet and you may choose comfortable walking shoes rather than boots, depending upon the time of year. With many places to stop for refreshments and shelter and good transport links, there is little use for a large and heavy backpack.

Leaving the Thames at Crayford Ness it can be muddy and once past Dartford we are into the countryside and boots and protective gear may be more appropriate.

The remaining sections are a mix of hard paths, country paths, bridleways and, after Staplehurst, mostly farmland. There are climbs and descents, walks through woodland and across fields and, especially after rain, the going can get heavy and muddy in places as travellers found in the 18th century.

You will not need 'expedition' wear unless you want to tackle 1066 Harold's Way in the depths of winter, in snow and with a force 10 gale blowing across the Downs and the Weald. For the rest of us it is best to take sensible boots or appropriate shoes and warm and waterproof clothing. The golden rule is, be comfortable, dress for the sort of weather and terrain you are likely to meet, and never underestimate the changeability of British weather!

Services and refreshment stops become more infrequent but there are pubs and villages along the walk. 1066 Harold's Way is new long distance walk and muddy boots may not be that welcome if you stop for a pint. All walkers and ramblers know that with boots off and packs off we are more likely to be fed and watered by 'mine host'. I hope that as 1066 Harold's Way becomes more popular so will be our welcome.

Footwear
- Boots for preference, shoes or lighter boots for the town sections.

Clothing
- Waterproof and wind proof wear and a fleece, it can be chilly on the Downs.
- Technical wear – jeans are not recommended by The Ramblers.
- Shorts if you prefer but long trousers offer better protection against brambles, nettles and sprayed crops etc and long trousers should be carried if weather changes are forecast.

Equipment
- Daypack.
- Maps and Harold's Way Guide.
- Compass / GPS. Signage and paths can be hidden or non–existent and knowing which direction to walk is invaluable and face saving.
- Water, snacks and/or thermos flask, adequate for your walk.
- Food, unless you're absolutely sure you'll be able to eat on the way.
- Extra clothing, especially in winter.
- Camera and/or a mobile phone.
- Spare laces.

Most walkers know the gear that suits them, through experience, but for those new to walking or with less experience of walking on the Downs, Weald and High Weald, the Ramblers offer advice at: www.ramblers.org.uk/info/practical/gear.htm

Transport

1066 Harold's Way is fully accessible by public transport and I found that the trains and buses served me well and negated the need for two cars and finding car parking, which in the larger towns was expensive and in villages, like Bodiam, non-existent.

1. If you are travelling by train and your return journey is back along the same line, you will find it more economic to buy a return ticket to the furthest station and get off early for your walk.

2. Many country bus routes also offer return tickets and similarly Note 1 will also apply if you are using the same route for the outward and return journeys.

The following links will help you plan your journey ahead of your walk.

Transport for London	www.tfl.gov.uk
Thames Clippers	www.thamesclippers.com
Traveline Journey Planner	www.travelinesoutheast.org.uk or
	Traveline on 0870 608 2608
Weather Forecast	www.news.bbc.co.uk/weather/
Tourist Information	www.information-britain.co.uk/tic.cfm

Footpaths and Footpath problems

The Ramblers' act to preserve our walking heritage and have a great website giving guidance and advice on all matters 'walking'. Membership provides additional benefits both for you and for the Association. (www.ramblers.org.uk). Local Authorities and County Councils, by necessity, have reduced resources to carry out surveys of the state of their path network and they rely on reports by path users.

Reporting problems can help to put them right and they can

be identified and reported online, through the Ramblers website. We do need to protect not just 1066 Harold's Way but the paths that we all enjoy using.

Fields can be ploughed out and footpaths not re-instated, even well used paths can be affected. Such problems should be reported but you will still be able to walk the path. If you are in a group, walk in single file so that the route is clearer. A path problem can be anything that spoils your enjoyment of a walk and may include:

Natural Vegetation:
- undergrowth
- overgrowth
- hedgerow encroachment
- overhanging branches
- fallen trees, etc.

Paths:
- 'furniture'
- missing or broken stiles
- bridges
- gates
- signposts
- waymarks

Miscellaneous:
- misleading notices
- dangerous animals
- surface problems, etc.

Agriculture Related:
- ploughing
- cropping
- manure
- slurry, etc.

Man-made Problems:
- barbed wire
- buildings
- fences
- walls
- rubbish
- rubble, etc.

You can make a report online to The Ramblers using the following link:

www.ramblers.org.uk/rights_of_way/volunteer_opportunities/ footpath_guardian_scheme/footpath_guardian_toolkit.htm

Rights of Way

Thousands of footpaths, many dating back centuries could be lost unless they are officially recorded as footpaths, bridleways or byways by 2026. Once a highway, always a highway but many 'lost routes' are at risk of losing their status. "These routes are part of our history, no other country has such a wonderful network of rights of way" Kate Ashbrook, Open Spaces Society (BBC Countryfile Magazine, Aug 2010). 1066

1066 Harold's Way uses some of these older routes and the continued walking of these paths will help confirm their status. However, some of the Roman roads appear to have already been 'lost' and maybe they could be resurrected for all our enjoyment. We walk in hope.

In London, individual footpaths, pavements, signing and most parks and open spaces are the responsibility of the London Borough Councils, and the Corporation of London in the City of London. All the boroughs are listed under Local Authorities. Some borough websites are excellent sources of information on local resources for walkers. Any problems on footpaths should be should be reported to the relevant Borough or County.

Road Walking

On the occasions when we need to walk on the road, there is some additional advice to consider:

- In the UK, on roads where there is no footpath, we would normally walk on the right facing the oncoming traffic.
- If you are walking in single file or in a group, it is important that those at the front and back wear clothing that is clearly visible to all traffic.
- At left bends, keep to the right.
- At right hand bends, consider crossing the road, in good time, to avoid any sudden encounters with oncoming traffic, who may not see you until the last minute. Cross back to the right hand side when it is safe to do so.
- I find that the majority of drivers do slow down, and / or give you a wider berth, with good humour and I do tend to acknowledge their kindness.

Thank you

You can help make 1066 Harold's Way safe for future walkers.

If there are any major alterations or changes to 1066 Harold's Way they will be advised through the website and facebook:

- www.1066haroldsway.co.uk
- facebook:1066haroldsway

The Code

www.countrysideaccess.gov.uk

- Be safe - plan ahead and follow any signs.
- For any walk, it's best to get the latest information about when and where you can go and any footpath updates and local diversions. Follow advice, local signs and be prepared for the unexpected. Refer to up-to-date maps or guidebooks.
- You're responsible for your own safety and perhaps for others within your group, so be prepared for changes in weather and other events. Check weather conditions before you leave, and don't be afraid to turn back.
- Part of the appeal of the countryside is that you can get away from it all. There are many places without clear mobile phone signals, so let someone know where you're going and when you expect to return.
- Leave gates and property as you find them.
- Please respect the working life of the countryside, as our actions can affect people's livelihoods, our heritage, and the safety and welfare of animals and ourselves.
- Leave gates as you find them or follow instructions on signs. If walking in a group, make sure the last person knows how to leave the gate.
- If you think a sign is illegal or misleading such as a 'Private - No Entry' sign on a public footpath, contact the local authority.
- In fields where crops are growing, follow the paths wherever possible.
- Use gates, stiles or gaps in field boundaries when provided - climbing over walls, hedges and fences can damage them and increase the risk of farm animals escaping.
- Protect plants and animals and take your litter home.
- We have a responsibility to protect our countryside now and for future generations, so make sure you don't harm animals, birds, plants or trees.
- Keep dogs under close control.
- The countryside is a great place to exercise dogs, but it's every owner's duty to make sure their dog is not a danger or nuisance to farm animals, wildlife or other people.
- Much of 1066 Harold's Way is through farmland devoted to sheep, cattle and horses and care is required for your safety as well.
- If a farm animal chases you and your dog, it is safer to let your dog off the lead – don't risk getting hurt by trying to protect it.
- You do not have to put your dog on a lead on public paths, as long as it is under close control. But as a general rule, keep your dog on a lead if you cannot rely on its obedience.
- Showing respect and consideration for other people makes the countryside a pleasant place for everyone and there is the opportunity to support the rural economy by using the local shops and businesses along Harold's Way.
- To help the environment, I use public transport for all of 1066 Harold's Way - each section highlights the local transport links.

APPENDIX 2:
DISTANCES AND TRAVEL LINKS

Place Name	Miles		Total	Time	Transport Links from path	Minutes/Miles
1. Westminster					Westminster	
London Bridge	2.50	2.50				
Tower Bridge	0.50	3.00				
The Mayflower PH	1.50	4.50				
Surrey Docks Farm	1.50	6.00				
Greenwich	3.00	9.00	9.00	180	Greenwich Station	10 / 0.5
2. Greenwich						
Meridian Post The O2 Arena	2.50	2.50				
Thames Barrier	2.00	4.50				
Plumstead Common	2.50	7.00				
Lesnes Abbey	2.75	9.75	18.75	210	Abbey Wood Station	10 / 0.5
3. Lesnes Abbey						
Erith	3.00	3.00				
Crayford Ness	2.00	5.00				
Dartford Station	4.75	9.75	28.50	210	Dartford Station	
4. Dartford Station						
Dartford High Street	0.50	0.50				
Darenth Parsonage Lane	2.50	3.00				
Betsham	3.50	6.50				
Southfleet Ship Inn	0.75	7.25				
Istead Rise Upper Avenue	2.00	9.25	37.75	210	Gravesend Station Bus 306/308	12 mins (bus)

5. Istead Rise Upper Avenue

Place						
Jeskyns Country Park	1.75	1.75				
Cobham	1.00	2.75				
Darnley Mausoluem	1.75	4.50				
Rochester Medway Bridge	4.25	8.75	46.50	180	Rochester Station	12 / 0.6

6. Rochester Medway Bridge

Place						
Nashenden Farm	2.50	2.50				
Robin Hood PH	2.25	4.75				
Bluebell Hill Car Park & Picnic Site	1.25	6.00				
Kit's Coty House	1.00	7.00				
Malta Inn, Allington Lock	2.80	9.80				
Maidstone, Archbishop's Palace	2.20	12.00	58.50	300	Maidstone Stations	10 / 0.5

7. Maidstone, Archbishop's Palace

Place						
Loose Village	2.75	2.75				
The Quarries	1.25	4.00				
Greensand Way	2.50	6.50				
Lord Raglan PH, Rabbit's Cross	1.50	8.00				
Staplehurst Station	2.50	10.50	69.00	240	Staplehurst Station Bus Arriva 5	

8. Staplehurst Station

Place						
Staplehurst Old Town	1.90	1.90				
Little Wadd Farm	2.50	4.40				
Knox Bridge	0.75	5.15				
Hocker Edge	2.00	7.15				
Sissinghurst Castle	2.25	9.40				
The Bull, Sissinghurst	1.25	10.65	79.65	240	Sissinghurst Bus Arriva 5	30 / 1.25

9. Sissinghurst The Bull

High Weald Landscape Trail	1.40	1.40			
Benenden School	1.90	3.30			
TQ816302 The Woodcock PH	1.80	5.10			
Sandhurst New Swan & Bus Stop	2.40	7.50			
Bodiam Castle	3.50	11.00	90.65	270	Bus Stagecoach 349

10. Bodiam Castle

Collier's Green	2.50	2.50			
Sedlescombe Queens Head	3.50	6.00			
Battle Abbey	3.25	9.25	99.90	210	See 10a

10a. Bodiam Castle

Collier's Green	2.50	2.50			
Miles Farm	1.00	3.50			
Cripps Corner	1.00	4.50			
Vinehall Street	2.20	6.70			
Battle Abbey	3.30	10.00	100.65	240	Bus Stagecoach 304 / 305
				Battle Station	10 / 0.5

Travel Links. For all travel requirements, connections, timetables and journey suggestions try:

Travel Line South East	www.travelinesoutheast.org.uk

Or

London Underground	www.tfl.gov.uk
Thames Clipper	www.thamesclippers.com
South Eastern Trains	www.southeasternrailway.co.uk
Stagecoach	www.stagecoachbus.com/hastings
Arriva	www.arrivabus.co.uk

1066 HAROLD'S WAY APPENDIX 3:
PUBS, INNS

Pubs and Inns

Listed at the following link are some of the many pubs and inns to stop for a drink along the way:

http://www.1066haroldsway.co.uk/Pages/PubsandInns.aspx

In some of the London pubs and bars, you may stand out a little from all the men and women in 'suits' but you will have a different story to talk about. Some may be a short walk from 1066 Harold's Way and for others, we may arrive a little too early in the day but they can still be a line in your little black, beer stained notebook with a note to return to later as I will on my future annual treks.

The Abbey Inn, Battle, is a convenient place to end the walk. The hotel offers snacks, meals and drinks as well rooms for the night.

1066 HAROLD'S WAY APPENDIX 4:
WEBLINKS AND ACCOMMODATION

The quick links to all the sites that have been mentioned in 1066 Harold's Way can be accessed at:
http://www.1066haroldsway.co.uk/Pages/WeblinksandAccommodation.aspx

Grouped together under the Walk headings they can be accessed directly from the Web page links by visiting www.1066haroldsway.co.uk.

Accommodation that I have passed along 1066 Harold's Way is shown under each Walk heading.

Any suggestions should not be viewed as endorsements and they are in no way to be seen as recommendations - you must be guided by your own instincts and judgement after all, your ideal accommodation may just be around the corner away from the walk.

There are many sources for general tourist information and accommodation in the bookshop and on the internet and to help I have also listed the links to the official Tourist Information sites below.

Note: The website links are correct as at December 2012 and are checked on a regular basis although addresses may change in the interim

1066 HAROLD'S WAY.
BIBLIOGRAPHY

Sources:

Roman Roads in Britain, Ivan D Margary
Roman Roads in Sussex, Alex Vincent
An Historical Atlas of Kent, ed.Lawson and Killingray
An Atlas of Roman Britain, Jones and Mattingly
An Historical Atlas of Sussex, ed.Leslie, Short and Rowland
The Kent and Sussex Weald, Peter Brandon
Walks into History, John Wilks
Kent and Sussex Battlefield Walks, Rupert Matthews
An Introduction to Anglo Saxon England, Peter Hunter Blair
1066 the Battles of York, Stamford Bridge and Hastings, Peter Marren
The Place Names of Kent, Judith Glover
Sussex Place Names, Judith Glover
The King's England, Arthur Mee
The Shell Guide to England, ed. John Hadfield
Sir John Sedley Charity, Ralph Penniston Taylor
Cobham Village Guide, revised May 2008 (I got my copy from the church cost £2)
The Hastings Hundreds, David Ingram
The 1066 Malfosse Walk, Compiled by Neil Clephane-Cameron, Joanne Lawrence and David Sawyer *Battle and District Historical Society*
The 1066 Country Walk, Brian Smails
50 Walks in Sussex, The AA
London Walks, Tom Pocock
Walk Britain 2010, The Ramblers
English Heritage Guide 2011
National Trust Guide 2011
Good Beer Guide 2010
The Pubs of London, RM Smith
Birmingham Roman Roads Project

Bretwalda Books Ltd